The Aesthetics
of the Greek Banquet

The Aesthetics
of the Greek Banquet

Images of Wine and Ritual
(*Un Flot d'Images*)

François Lissarrague

Translated by Andrew Szegedy-Maszak

PRINCETON UNIVERSITY PRESS

Princeton, New Jersey

Originally published as
Un Flot d'Images: une esthétique du banquet grec
© 1987, Editions Adam Biro, Paris, France

Copyright © 1990 by Princeton University Press
Published by Princeton University Press, 41 William Street,
Princeton, New Jersey 08540
In the United Kingdom: Princeton University Press, Oxford

Library of Congress Cataloging-in-Publication Data

Lissarrague, F. (François)
[Flot d'images. English]
The aesthetics of the Greek banquet: Images of Wine and Ritual / by François
Lissarrague : translated by Andrew Szegedy-Maszak.

p.   cm.
Translation of· Un flot d'images.
ISBN 0-691-03595-4 (alk. paper) :
1. Vase-painting, Greek. 2. Dinners and dining in art.
3. Aesthetics, Ancient. 4. Greece—Social life and customs—Pictorial works. I.
Title.
NK4645.L5713 1990
738.3'82'0938—dc20   89-70263

Publication of this book has been aided by a grant from the
Paul Mellon Fund of Princeton University Press

This book has been composed in Linotron Garamond

Princeton University Press books are printed on acid-free
paper, and meet the guidelines for permanence and
durability of the Committee on Production Guidelines
for Book Longevity of the Council on Library Resources

Printed in the United States of America by
Princeton University Press, Princeton, New Jersey

10 9 8 7 6 5 4 3 2 1

Contents

Abbreviations Used in the Notes

Beazley, ABV: J. D. Beazley, *Attic Black-Figure Vase-Painters*. Oxford, 1956.

Beazley, ARV: J. D. Beazley, *Attic Red-Figure Vase-Painters*. Oxford, 1963.

CVA: *Corpus Vasorum Antiquorum* (followed by the number of the fascicle and the plate by city and, between parentheses, by the numbers of the fascicle and the plate by country).

The Aesthetics
of the Greek Banquet

Chapter 1

The Greek Experience of Wine

When speaking about wine, the Greeks were inexhaustible. Drinkers' dialogues, experts' discussions, lyric poems, and mythological tales—the literature that deals with the divine beverage is extensive.[1] Given such abundance it is difficult to account for every detail, but we can isolate certain basic concepts, within Greek culture, regarding the use, the origin, and the value of wine.

In the *Bacchae* Euripides dramatizes the vast power of Dionysus. At several points the god of wine is described as the one who has given mortals the cure for their sorrows, forgetfulness (in the sleep that follows drinking) of their cares, and relief for their suffering. The chorus sings his praise:

> . . . the prince of the blessèd,
> the god of garlands and banquets,
> Bromius, Semele's son . . .

[1] Plutarch, *Table Talk*; Athenaeus, *Deipnosophists*. I will refer to the following modern studies: R. Billiard, *La vigne et le vin dans l'Antiquité* (Lyon, 1913); G. Hagenow, *Aus dem Weingarten der Antike* (Mayence, 1982). On the religious use of wine, see K. Kirchner, *Die sakrale Bedeutung des Weines im Altertum* (Giessen, 1910). On drunkenness, see P. Villard, *Recherches sur l'ivresse dans le monde grec; vocabulaire, physiologie* (diss., Aix-en-Provence, 1975). Finally, on the iconography of the symposion, see B. Fehr, *Orientalische und griechische Gelage* (Bonn, 1971); J. M. Dentzer, *Le Motif du banquet couché dans le Proche-Orient et le monde grec du VIIe au IVe siècle av. J.-C.* (Rome, 1982).

These blessings he gave:
laughter to the flute
and the loosing of cares
when the shining wine is spilled
at the feast of the gods,
and the wine-bowl casts its sleep
on feasters crowned with ivy.[2]

Moreover, his blessings belong to all, without distinction; Dionysus is a true democrat:

The deity, the son of Zeus,
in feast, in festival, delights.
He loves the goddess Peace,
generous of good,
preserver of the young.
To rich and poor he gives
the simple gift of wine,
the gladness of the grape.[3]

Wine as an anodyne is one of the images most familiar to us; throughout our tradition "wine dissolves sorrow"—it is an artificial paradise, a drug that alleviates pain.

This depiction does appear in Greece—the *Bacchae* is only one instance among many[4]—but it is not so pervasive as it is in our modern imagination. The idea of wine as a release is actually a secondary aspect in the Greek world view. There wine is thought of as a blessing, a divine gift of major importance, equivalent to Demeter's gift of grain. The prophet Teiresias offers the following explanation to Pentheus, the young king of Thebes, who refuses to welcome Dionysus into his city:

Mankind, young man, possesses two supreme blessings.
First of these is the goddess Demeter, or Earth—
whichever name you choose to call her by.
It was she who gave to man his nourishment of grain.
But after her came the son of Semele,

[2] Euripides, *Bacchae*, 375–385, trans. Arrowsmith.
[3] Euripides, *Bacchae*, 416–423, trans. Arrowsmith.
[4] Cf. Alcaeus in Athenaeus, 10.430c–d (= fr. Z22 Lobel-Page).

4

who matched her present by inventing liquid wine
as his gift to man. For filled with that good gift,
suffering mankind forgets its grief; from it
comes sleep; with it oblivion of the troubles
of the day. There is no other medicine for misery.[5]

Wine is seen as a positive force whose activity is not restricted
to the temporary suppression of evil, of all the misery inherent to
the human condition; rather, its use is put in a religious context,
just like that of grain. All city-states took care to pass laws on its
use, some very few—like Sparta—to proscribe its use by citizens,
most to regulate it.

Such control was necessary because, in the Greek imagination, wine is an ambiguous drink, like liquid fire, at once dangerous
and beneficial. The myths that tell of the origin of the vine and of
wine highlight their ambivalent nature, halfway between the savage
and the civilized, functioning as a mediation between these two po-
lar opposites. The grapevine has its origin outside the world of man:
according to the stories, it came from a root fallen from the sky,[6] or
was found by a goat (an animal that is half-wild and half-domesti-
cated),[7] or perhaps brought in by a bitch, according to a version that
blurs the distinction between animals and plants.[8] Conversely,
wine—after the process of vinification, which is conceived of as
cooking—is located on the side of culture, of a complex technical
skill that differentiates it from fruit and produce. Dionysus shares
in this doubleness: in his link to plant life and the spreading vine
(see fig. 94),[9] he is marked by exuberance; but he is nonetheless the
master over wine and its effects. The Athenian religious calendar
emphasizes the latter aspect; the festivals of Dionysus are not connected with the grape harvest, and he does not seem to be considered
a god of agriculture. The new wine and the opening of the storage

[5] Euripides, *Bacchae*, 274–283, trans. Arrowsmith.
[6] Nonnos, *Dionysiaca*, 12.193ff.
[7] Mythographi Vaticani, 1.87.
[8] Pausanias, 10.38.1; Athenaeus, 2.35b.
[9] See H. Jeanmaire, *Dionysos, histoire du culte de Bacchus* (Paris, 1951), 12–18; and,
especially, W. Otto, *Dionysus: Myth and Cult*, trans. R. Palmer (Bloomington,
Ind., 1965), 143–159.

jars occasioned the most important ceremonies in January-February.[10] The miracle of wine, annually repeated and celebrated under the auspices of Dionysus, is a dangerous moment in the etiological myths. The effects of the first wine are always devastating: the first men to taste it go mad, think themselves possessed, and kill the one who made them drink it.[11]

In fact, wine is a poison, but Dionysus gives it to men along with the rules for its use. It teaches the Athenians about mixture, the proportions involved in blending. Wine, indeed, is fundamentally linked to mixing; in the ancient world it is drunk only when blended with water. This custom is certainly due to its high alcohol content, which in turn is due to a late harvest, after the leaves have fallen. At that point, says Cato, the grape is *percoctus*, "quite cooked."[12] The liquor it yields, if drunk neat, is a drug that can madden or kill,[13] a true *pharmakon* in the double meaning of the Greek term: both poison and medicine. The medicinal use of wine is widely attested.[14] The pure essence is called *akratos*, unmixed. This linguistic fact is very significant because it illuminates the essential quality of wine that makes it fit to drink: mixture. Pure wine—for us the only drinkable kind—is defined in Greek by a negative term formed from the alpha-privative and the word *kratos* (whence the name of the vase, *krater*), which denotes a mingling. Modern Greek has preserved this word in calling wine *krasi*. Identification of wine with a process of mixing reappears in Artemidorus' *Oneirokritikos (Key to Dreams)*, which specifies that it is good "for someone planning to marry or to contract an alliance" to dream of a grapevine or wine, "the vine because of its intertwinings, wine because it is mixed."[15]

[10] On these festivals, see L. Deubner, *Attische Feste* (Berlin, 1932), 93–151; Jeanmaire, *Dionysos*, 36–56.

[11] Apollodoros, 3.14.7 (the story of Icarios).

[12] Cato, *De agricultura*, 28 (25); the word can also mean a swarthy coloring, as at Lucretius, 6.722. In Greek we find a similar play on *aithops* and *aithiops*; see J.-P. Vernant, *La cuisine du sacrifice en pays grec* (Paris, 1979), 247.

[13] See, for example, the story of the centaur Eurytion, *Od.*, 21.295ff.; also, Athenaeus, 10.437a.

[14] J. Pigeaud, *La maladie de l'âme* (Paris, 1981), 477–503.

[15] Artemidorus, 4.3, 224.

Among the regulations connected with wine, those established by Lycurgus at Sparta, as reported by Plutarch, are particularly interesting because they address the use of pure wine in its application as an analytic tool.[16] Newborn infants are dipped into pure wine to detect cases of epilepsy; those that have the disease go into convulsions. Here wine serves as an instrument of selection. Another use of wine can be classified as educational: we know that at Sparta the helots, the serfs who were tied to the land and constituted the lower class of society, were made to drink pure wine and then led, drunk, into the city. There they sang obscene songs accompanied by indecent dances, in order to instill in the Spartan youths a horror of the wine that caused such reprehensible behavior. In both these cases pure wine is defined as a drug whose use indicates complete alienation: it excludes the unworthy newborn, rejected from the time of birth, and it signals the total otherness of the inferiors who are treated like animals.

In all of Greece, drinking unmixed wine is a barbarian custom, summed up in the proverbial expression "to drink like a Scythian." King Cleomenes of Sparta died a madman from having drunk too much pure wine in the company of Scythian envoys.[17] Wine and its mixing are universal cultural indicators, and the whole imagery of wine in ancient Greece is constellated around such mixing. This image in turn gives rise to a vastly greater set of fundamental social, religious, and philosophical ideas.

This point deserves to be underscored: in the process of mixing the proportions might vary but are never left to chance. The crucial instrument is the krater, the great vessel that we see so often placed on the floor amidst the guests at a symposion (see fig. 11).[18] The latter word, often translated as "banquet," actually means the moment when people drink together; people do not eat at the symposion because it generally takes place after the actual meal. It is a social gathering that brings together adult male citizens; among themselves they drink, sing lyric poetry, play music, and converse on various topics. A fragment of a drinking-song hints at the spirit,

[16] Plutarch, *Lycurgus*, 16.3, 28.8. Of course this is a reconstruction of a model that may well be a utopia, but it still holds great interest for a historian of ideas.
[17] Herodotus, 6.84.
[18] For the symposion, see chap. 2.

and almost the agenda, of such meetings, as it reiterates the prefix *syn-* ("with"), an essential term that marks the symposion's ideal of community and conviviality: "Drink with me, play music with me, love with me, wear a crown with me, be mad with me when I am mad and wise with me when I am wise."[19]

At the symposion one can pass from wisdom to folly; the option remains open. On each occasion rules are passed under the aegis of the master of the banquet, the symposiarch, whom the guests must obey.[20] He prescribes the musical themes, or the topic of conversation; in Plato's *Symposium*, for example, after Eryximachos has dismissed the flute girl, he suggests that each guest in turn offer a speech in praise of Love.[21] The symposiarch also decides the number of kraters that will be drunk, as well as the ratio of water to wine, which can vary from 3:1 to 5:3 or 3:2, depending on the desired strength of the mixture.[22] These proportions are thought of as harmonic balances, almost like music; thus Plutarch tells of a drinker who describes a good mixture as being like a chord and is then jokingly invited to take his cup as he would pick up his lyre, in order to drink like a good musician.[23]

Within the framework of the symposion, the use of wine is the basis for a set of practices that define the symposion as a process, an experience both positive and necessary for social life. We can distinguish several levels in this process. To begin with, wine is an agent for sociability, a means for bringing things to light. The lyric poets, whose verses were recited or sung during the banquets and who were often poets of wine, alluded to this phenomenon in many passages that present wine as something that reveals the truth. Alcaeus links the two in a kind of proverb, "Wine and truth [*in vino veritas*]." Theognis is more explicit:

> It is in fire that experts test gold and silver;
> It is wine that discloses the soul of a man.[24]

---

[19] Carmina convivalia, 19/902 Page (Athenaeus, 15.695d).
[20] Plutarch, *Table Talk*, 1.4.620a–622b.
[21] Plato, *Symposium*, 176e and 177d.
[22] Hesiod, *Works and Days*, 596; Athenaeus, 10.423–427; Plutarch, *Table Talk*, 3.9. See also D. Page, *Sappho and Alcaeus* (Oxford, 1979), 308.
[23] Plutarch, *Table Talk*, 3.9.2.657d.
[24] Alcaeus, fr. Z43 Lobel-Page (cf. fr. Z9); Theognis, 499–500.

In a vivid image, Aeschylus explains: "Bronze reflects the appearance; wine is the mirror of the soul."[25]

In the *Laws* Plato emphasizes the revelatory aspect of wine. In the course of this long dialogue in which he sets himself up as legislator for a utopian city, the philosopher often seems drawn to the Spartan model that prohibited symposia and instead adopted *syssitia*, compulsory meals taken in common that were exemplary in their austerity and temperance. But in this case Plato abandons his model. Far from banning wine from his city, he defends and justifies the symposion. He claims that wine can disclose another's character without the slightest danger.[26] To discover if one is dealing with someone violent, unjust, brutal, or addicted to the pleasures of love, it is much better to associate with him during communal drinking than to risk endangering one's wife or son or daughter.

Everything takes place as if the symposion were the site of a simulated experience and wine were the agent of this simulation. The experience remains free of danger because it is controlled by the symposiarch, the master of ceremonies, who is compared to a general without whom it is dangerous to go to war. Disobeying his orders results in exclusion from the banquets, hence social isolation. For Plato this testing by means of wine has an educational goal; it means that one comes to know individual characters in their true nature, in order to be able to make them better. As regards moderation, a primary virtue, such improvement is accomplished through the medium of wine. One can learn temperance only through drunkenness; related to the golden mean, temperance is equated with the right mixture.

This ideal of a wise balance in the use of wine is already clear in Theognis:

> Wine drunk in excess is an evil; if we drink it wisely (*episthēmōs*) it is not an evil but a blessing. Drinking brings down on frail men two great dangers: parching thirst, and disabling drunkenness. I place myself between these two extremes, and you will not persuade me either to stop drinking, or to become riotously drunk.[27]

---

[25] Aeschylus *ap.* Athenaeus, 10.427f (= fr. 393 N²).

[26] Plato, *Laws*, 649d–650b. See P. Boyancé, "Platon et le vin," BAGB, *Lettres d'humanité* (1951), 3–19.

[27] Theognis, 509–510, 837–840. On Theognis, see the collection of articles ed-

Greek morality, which idealizes balance (but neither frustration nor self-denial), is conceived on the model of the correct mixture of wine and water and linked to the image of the krater.

This is more than a matter of prudence and unreflective moderation. For the Greeks wine allows experience at another level: not only of another person, a neighbor, a drinking companion, but also of an otherness that each person feels in his own liberation and self-emancipation. Wine, says Plato, confers a sense of happiness, power, and freedom. For the latter he offers a specific example, which might seem commonplace but is a good illustration of how wine's action is viewed. In the *Laws* he makes rules for the use of wine according to the age divisions.[28] Prior to the age of eighteen, children are not to drink it because "they must not add fuel to the fire in their souls." Up to the age of thirty, the citizens may drink in moderation, with absolutely no excess or drunkenness. Thereafter, in their forties, they may "invite Dionysus" to "relieve the dessication of old age." Thus wine becomes a necessity for the mature adult; his rigid spirit has to "soften, like iron thrust into the fire." Wine warms the soul and removes its stiffness, just as it removes its worries. The action of wine, however, is not just negative; it has a positive effect in making the old man happy in his life and newly sociable. His soul, once again as pliable as that of a child, can be reshaped, and this malleability has a direct effect during religious observances: it allows the old man to sing and to dance, which are important social activities. At festivals each age class has to perform appropriate songs and dances, which have a pronounced moral efficacy. Without the assistance of wine, the adult males would not be able to give up their caution, the reserve that befits their age. Their experience is most valuable for the city, and—once the wine warms them up—they can sing and dance, and thereby fulfill their role and convey their message to others.

Plato's ideas might make us smile, but they give a very clear indication of how wine's power is understood: it frees us from restrictions, prohibitions, habits; it allows for a brief excursion outside

ited by T. Figueira and G. Nagy, *Theognis of Megara: Poetry and the Polis* (Baltimore, 1985).
[28] Plato, *Laws*, 666a–d.

normal boundaries. Old men recover the liveliness and sociability of youth. In contexts other than the Platonic, the excursion outside oneself takes the form of approaching the Other, not only the neighbor and fellow citizen but even the foreigner, the Other whose exclusion forms the basis for the structure of the state. In Athens as in Sparta, the citizen is defined by equality and identity. Full Spartan citizens are *Homoioi*, social and civic peers. The fundamental principle in Athens is *isonomia*, in which all citizens are equal before the law; such equality does not apply to women, slaves, or foreigners.[29]

In the experience of the symposion, imagery plays an important role. The vases used for drinking are not merely containers, or vessels for the consumption of wine; they are vehicles for images. Therefore the pictorial representations allow us to develop an iconography of wine, in which all the values we have discerned are embodied and organized in visual form.

Thus the search for otherness, the extraordinary but necessary experience of the Other, is expressed in the symposion by the portrayal of men dressed in women's clothing or costumed in Scythian style. On one vase, six young men are reclining in a circle, talking and raising their cups (fig. 1).[30] One of them is playing the *aulos*, the double-flute. He is wearing a Scythian headdress, which distinguishes him from his companions and marks him as a man apart, a peerless drinker. In the same way a whole set of images of a *komos*—a procession of drinkers on their way to or from a banquet—show men in women's attire.[31] On one krater, three such men make their way, garbed in long dresses, wearing women's caps (*sakkos*) and earrings (fig. 2).[32] Their maleness is indicated only by their beards, and their pose—at once feminine and oriental—clearly puts them in the

[29] See P. Vidal-Naquet, *The Black Hunter*, trans. A. Szegedy-Maszak (Baltimore, 1986), 1–12.

[30] Red-figure cup: New York, 16.174–41; Beazley, ARV 355/35.

[31] See F. Frontisi-Ducroux and F. Lissarrague, "From Ambiguity to Ambivalence: A Dionysiac Excursion through the 'Anakreontic' Vases," in *Before Sexuality*, ed. D. Halperin, J. Winkler, and F. Zeitlin (Princeton, N.J., 1990), 211–256; D. C. Kurtz and J. Boardman, "Booners," *Greek Vases in the J. Paul Getty Museum* 3 (1986): 35–70.

[32] Red-figure krater; Cleveland, 26.549; Beazley, ARV 563/9.

1. Red-figure cup, Colmar painter, ca. 500.

2. Red-figure krater, Pig Painter, ca. 480.

3. Red-figure cup, signed Epiktetos, ca. 510.

category of the nonmasculine. In the controlled context of the komos and the symposion, one can play the Other, for a while.

In the Athenian imagination, the experience that promotes
the escape of one's identity into otherness culminates—especially in
visual imagery—in the representation of satyrs; these are the half-
human, half-animal creatures that comprise Dionysus's male retinue. Their hybrid, bestial appearance is like an expression of that
radically Other element buried deep within every civilized man,
which drinking can bring to light, and which must be recognized
and tested. Thus there develop two levels of imagery concerning the
rituals of wine, one among humans, the other among the satyrs
around Dionysus. We will have frequent occasion to compare these
two sets, of which the latter reflects or reverses the former.

Consider, for example, a cup signed by the painter Epictetos:[33] it shows a figure who is bearded and snub nosed, with a horse's
ears and tail, reclining against a cushion (fig. 3). It is a satyr in the

[33] Red-figure cup; Baltimore; Beazley, ARV 75/56.

pose of a drinker at a symposion, but he is guzzling from a huge amphora. Here all the rules of decorous drinking are ignored: there is no mixture, no sharing with other guests; not even a drinking cup, but pure wine taken straight from the amphora used to store it. These are the manners of a satyr, a reckless, untamed drinker, always lured by the aroma of wine.

The same scent guides old Silenus in Euripides' *Cyclops*, when Odysseus disembarks on the giant's island where the satyrs are being held captive. Odysseus is carrying a full wineskin, and Silenus, who has endured a long abstinence, greets him with open arms:

> SILENUS: Where is the wine? On board ship? You have it?
> ODYSSEUS: In this flask, old man. Look for yourself.
> SILENUS: That? That wouldn't make one swallow for me.
> ODYSSEUS: No? For each swallow you take, the flask gives two.
> SILENUS: A fountain among fountains, that! I *like* it!
> ODYSSEUS: Will you have it unwatered to start with? . . .
> SILENUS: Pour away. A drink will joggle my memory.
> ODYSSEUS: There you are.
> SILENUS: Mmmmmm. Gods, what a bouquet![34]

Once again it is the bouquet, the passion for wine, that leads Silenus to disaster in his adventure at the court of King Midas. The Phrygian ruler, having learned that Silenus knew the secret of happiness, wanted to capture him and drag the information out of him. So he transformed a fountain into a fountain of wine; Silenus, drawn by the smell, went to drink there and was caught.[35] This episode appears on a *lekythos*, or flask (fig. 4).[36] The satyr is lying down with his face turned toward the miraculous fountainhead; meanwhile, above him an archer in an oriental cap creeps toward him, carrying the cord with which he will snare him. The scene is framed by two ornamental seated figures, one of whom might be King Midas. The fountain has become a trap. By contrast, on another lekythos (fig. 5) the fountain is supernatural;[37] it spews wine in abundance to fill

---

[34] Euripides, *Cyclops*, 145–153, trans. Arrowsmith.
[35] Xenophon, *Anabasis*, 1.2.13; Pausanias, 1.4.5; cf. M. Hubbard, "The Capture of Silenus," *PCPhS* 21 (1975): 53–62.
[36] Black-figure lekythos; London 1910.2–12; Beazley, ABV 507/32.
[37] Black-figure lekythos; Göttingen, ZV 1964/139; Beazley, *Para* 215, *Addenda* 57.

4. Black-figure lekythos, Sappho painter, ca. 490.

5. Black-figure lekythos, Gela painter, ca. 500.

15

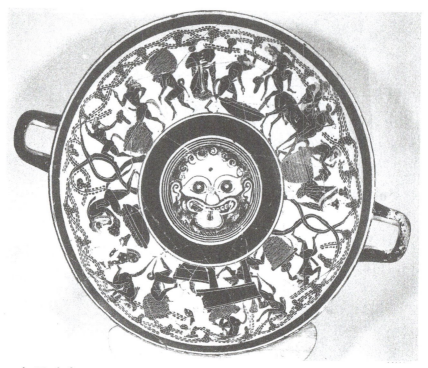

6. Black-figure cup, ca. 500.

an enormous *pithos*, a half-buried storage jar whose neck extends above ground and around which satyrs are capering. Trap or miracle, the wine pours out in streams, and the ambiguity of its nature, happy or hurtful, is readily apparent as we compare these two images.

Both the close connection between Dionysus and the vine and the power of the god over the production of wine are frequently represented on the vases. Dionysus often presides over the grape harvest and the pressing. In the tondo of a cup in the Cabinet des Médailles there is the grimacing face of a gorgon (fig. 6).[38] The surrounding band is occupied by a complex, fragmentary scene that juxtaposes several stages in the processing of the grapes. Next to the handles a pair of intertwined roots climbs up and extends its tendrils around the edge of the vase. Scattered through the branches, about a dozen satyrs bustle in every direction, filling large trays and wicker

[38] Black-figure cup; Paris, Cabinet des médailles, 320; Beazley, ABV 389.

7. Black-figure amphora, ca. 510.

baskets with enormous clusters of grapes. Several female figures accompany them. Under the gorgon's chin is a wine press; a satyr is stamping the grapes, whose juice runs into a bowl, while one of his impatient companions is stretched out under the press with his mouth agape, as if to intercept the liquor. Dionysus, crowned with ivy and seated on a mule, presides over this joyful harvest. Valuable as it is for historians of agriculture, such an image has little realism despite the precision of its details. There is no feeling of toil; rather than show human labor, the painter has preferred the imaginary world of the satyrs and the tireless activity of this Dionysiac band, which does not work but dances around Dionysus.[39] The association of Dionysus/vine/wine is often indicated by a simple juxtaposition of painted images. On a black-figure amphora (fig. 7),[40] the god is seated beside a huge vase, and between them there grows an inter-

[39] On this type of scene, see B. Sparkes, "Treading the Grapes," *BABesch* 51 (1976): 47–64.
[40] Black-figure amphora; Würzburg, 208; E. Langlotz, *Griechische Vasen in Würzburg* (Munich, 1932), pl. 44.

laced double root, which climbs upward to spread its branches, laden with heavy bunches of grapes, to cover the whole pictorial field. A satyr dances on the lip of the pithos and turns back toward the god, while another satyr approaches from the right carrying a pointed amphora. Dionysus holds a drinking vase with tall vertical handles, a *kantharos*. The image is focused around this unusually shaped vase, typical of the god,[41] which is placed between a cluster of grapes and the vessel where the wine is stored. The cup that belongs to the god visually draws the connection between the grape and the wine, without there being a depiction of the technical processes—harvesting, pressing, vinification—that make possible the passage from one state to the other.

The direct relation of the plant to the drink is shown by Dionysus's vase—sometimes a two-handled kantharos, sometimes a drinking horn (*rhyton*)—which becomes a specific iconographic attribute of the god, like a symbol of the power of Dionysus, the master and distributor of wine and drunkenness. The imagery on the vases generally highlights this function of Dionysus who, elsewhere in Greek cult, is not solely the god of wine;[42] on the vases, however, he is almost always portrayed near a vine, holding his drinking vase. By itself this object defines the god and all the values of wine that are attributed to him.

A final detail: in his account of Athens, Pausanias, the Greek traveler of the third century A.D., says that the Kerameikos, the potters' quarter, "is so named because of Keramos, son of Dionysus and Ariadne."[43] The rich get richer! Not only is the god the master of wine, he is also indirectly connected with the production of vases; therefore, under the patronage of Dionysus's son, painters and potters make the god of wine a major figure in the canon of visual images.

[41] See T. Carpenter, *Dionysian Imagery in Archaic Greek Art* (Oxford, 1986), 1, n. 1. On this type of vase, see the recent article by M. Gras, "Canthare, société étrusque et monde grec," *Opus* 3 (1984): 325–339.

[42] The literature on Dionysus is as profuse and varied as the god it discusses. In addition to the works by Jeanmaire and Otto (see n. 9), see the following recent studies: C. Kerényi, *Dionysos* (London, 1976); M. Daraki, *Dionysos* (Paris, 1985); M. Detienne, *Dionysos à ciel ouvert* (Paris, 1986) (Eng. trans.: *Dionysos at Large*, trans. A. Goldhammer [Cambridge, Mass., 1989]).

[43] Pausanias, 1.3.1.

Chapter 2

The Space of
the *Krater*

The Greeks are not solitary drinkers; the consumption of wine is seen as a communal act.[1] The symposion is organized as a community, with its own rules intended to establish a setting of shared pleasure.[2] One goes there in order to join a group temporarily defined by its manner of drinking, of blending wine and water. To be successful, the symposion strives for a good mixture, not only of liquids but also of guests, who will harmonize with one another like the strings of an instrument. The mixture also includes balanced and varied delights: drinks, perfumes, songs, music, dancing, games, conversation.[3] The symposion looks like a meeting with a changeable agenda, at once spectacle, performance, and enjoyment, with an appeal to all the senses: hearing, taste, touch, smell, and sight.

In the banquet hall, everyone is positioned so as to see all the others and to be on the same level as his companions, within range of sight and speech, so that conversation may flow easily. The couches are set up along the walls. Nothing, therefore, takes place behind the drinkers; the whole visual space is constructed to make sightlines converge and to ensure reciprocity. Each drinker has another alongside him or in front of him. Archaeological excavations

---

[1] There is an exception, on a black-figure skyphos; coll. Bareiss 337, J. Paul Getty Museum, S.80.AE 304; Basel, M.u.M. *Auktion* 34, no. 169.
[2] On this idea, see F. Dupont, *Le plaisir et la loi* (Paris, 1977), 26–36.
[3] Plutarch, *Table Talk*, 1.4.621b–e.

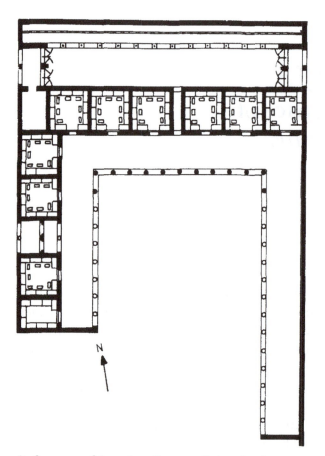

8. Sanctuary of Artemis at Brauron, dining chambers.

have given us an understanding of these rooms, which are never very big. At some shrines where religious festivals occasioned large communal feasts, it seems certain that the rooms were not made larger; rather, there were more of them. So it is at the sanctuary of Artemis at Brauron: nine rooms of equal size open onto a long portico, and each has room for eleven couches (fig. 8).[4]

This architectural space often has its graphic equivalent on

[4] See the plans reproduced in C. Boerker, *Festbankett und griechische Architektur* (Constance, 1983); for Brauron, his fig. 19, according to the reconstruction of C. Bouras, *He anastylosis tes stas tes Brauronos* (1967), 21, fig. 5. There is an excellent discussion in P. Schmitt-Pantel, "Le Cadre des banquets," in *La Cité au banquet* (diss. Lyon, 1987), 393–437.

9. Red-figure cup, Makron; signed Hieron potter, ca. 480.

the vases that depict a symposion. On one cup signed by the potter Hieron (*hieron epoesen*) there are arranged six couches with their occupants (fig. 9).[5] On one side, to the left, appears a bearded man with his hand on the shoulder of a half-naked woman, who is spinning a cup off the end of her finger.[6] In front of the couch is set a low table holding some wreaths; there is no food, since this is no longer the time for eating, but for drinking. In the center of the picture, in front of a bearded guest who has cup in his hand, stands

[5] Red-figure cup; New York, 20–246; Beazley, ARV 467/118.
[6] This gesture echoes the game of kottabos; see chap. 4 and figs. 67–72.

a female flute player. To the right the image is more fragmentary: a standing woman averts her eyes as she holds the head of someone who is vomiting into a large container on the ground; this is not a unique occurrence in Attic iconography, since the painters sometimes do show the excesses and debauchery of a banquet (see fig. 77).[7] A basket is suspended at the edge of the image. The other side shows the same arrangement of three couches with their small tables. Each couch is occupied by a reclining, bearded male. The one on the left is alone; in front of him a nude woman—her clothing is hung on the wall—is undoing the fillet that binds her hair. On the two other couches women lie next to the drinkers; the one to the right is spinning her cup like her companion on the other side. Next to them is a pair of castanets (*krotala*), like the ones dancers use. Between the two couches there is a stand with a small burning lamp on top; a ladle and a filter are hanging below it. The figure who appears under one handle holds the same kind of filter, as well as a pitcher in his other hand: this is a cup bearer, a *pais*, whose size denotes his age and status. The word "pais" has the same ambiguity as the French *garçon* or the English "boy," which can refer both to a child and to a slave. Pictorially this pais is symmetrically balanced with the large krater under the other handle: server and serving vessel are both indispensable props for the symposion.

In this picture all the ingredients of the symposion are present: wine, in the krater and in the drinking cups held by the guests; music, in the person of the flute player, and dance, implied by the castanets; and finally eros, embodied in the several female companions. The men are the central actors in this scene, each on his own couch, arranged without hierarchy in a circle. Woman plays a secondary, quasi-instrumental role: whether as musician, lover, or nursemaid to the sick drinker, she is almost as much an accessory for the symposion as is the great krater. The depiction gives a clear sense of the quality of this meeting: a male gathering, where there is an assortment of pleasures—wine, music, sex—and where conversation is represented by the play of glances and gestures that convey the exchanges between the guests and their partners. The spatial

[7] See E. Knauer, "Ou gar en amis," *Greek Vases in the J. Paul Getty Museum* 2 (1985): 91–100, and the red-figure cup, Brussels, R259; Beazley, ARV 169/7.

10. Red-figure stamnos, Smikros, ca. 510.

organization of the painted figures on the outside of the cup is equally significant: the circle of drinkers corresponds to the curved surface of the vase. Under the handles, the krater and its opposite number, the young boy, are not marginalized; they must be put in their proper place, at the center of the celebration. In fact, at a symposion the krater constitutes the focal point for the group; it is the shared cup, the vessel that contains the essential reaction, the mixing of water and wine.

Nevertheless, the actual process of mixing only rarely engages the painters' attention. One example appears on a *stamnos*—another type of mixing bowl[8]—where a youth and a bearded man busy themselves around a large *dinos* (a kind of krater without handles) on an elaborate stand (fig. 10). Each wears a loincloth knotted at the waist and carries a pointed amphora, of the type used to transport wine. In this image there is no water jug; only the wine matters. On the ground there are two pitchers which will be used to distribute the wine to the guests depicted on the other side of the vase. This picture, without any sign of the proportions of mixing, is dedicated to the activities of filling and sharing.

Indeed, the painters are most interested in the serving of wine, as it is passed among the guests. On another stamnos we find a woman with a pitcher (*oenochoe*) in her hand, going to refill the cup

[8] Red-figure stamnos; Brussels, A717; Beazley, ARV 20/1. See also the red-figure hydria; Rome, Vatican G71; Beazley, ARV 20/14; in addition, there is a red-figure cup; Heidelberg, 61; Beazley, ARV 144/1.

11. Red-figure stamnos,
Copenhagen painter, ca. 480.

extended toward her by a bearded male guest (fig. 11).[9] This woman occupies the center of the image. She stands between two couches, before which, as usual, there are two tables. The latter are loaded with shapeless objects, which must be cakes or snacks of some kind.[10] Under the table there hangs a basket that could have been used to carry the food or the various drinking cups. The scene is identical on the other side: two couches, with two revelers, one bearded and one not. Thus youths and adults are linked in this image, which is arranged as a continuous frieze around the whole vase.

[9] Red-figure stamnos; Oxford, 1965.127; Beazley, ARV 258/21; 1640.
[10] This is my translation for the Greek *tragemata*, to which Athenaeus devotes part of Book 14 (640c–658c).

The painted surface is not circular but cylindrical; still, like the earlier example, the space is pictorially constructed as an uninterrupted circle. It is worth noting that this image appears on a stamnos, and that a krater appears under one of the handles—twice removed, a vase painted on a vase. By imagining this krater among the drinkers, we find something like a reverse symmetry, a mirror image, between the drinkers in the hall and their depiction on the krater. The pictorial surface is cylindrical, hence centrifugal, while the couches in the room are arranged so that they converge. The image sends the guests a reflection of their own activity.

Moreover, on this stamnos the krater located under one handle has its symmetrical corollary under the other handle: it is an altar, a solid block of stone decorated with a frieze, yet there is nothing on top of it and there is no fire to indicate a sacrifice in progress.[11] Lodged firmly in the ground, the altar is a fixed point in domestic space as in sacred space. It is there that animals are sacrificed to the gods, before being cut up and shared among the humans during the meal that precedes the symposion. The presence of an altar in this painting recalls this earlier stage of the banquet, but without showing the sacrifice, which is only suggested. In any event, the altar denotes the tie that binds mortals and gods and underscores the ritual nature of this symposion. In its symmetry with the krater, it endows the latter with the quasi-architectural meaning of a communal object around which is organized the ritual consumption of wine.

We must take the word "ritual" seriously. The symposion is a social ritual in the broadest sense, in that it comprises a series of acts that are strictly codified and ordered prior to their accomplishment. More to the point, it includes a ritual component that is truly religious, in the dedication to the gods of part of the wine that is to be drunk; in Greek this is the libation (*spondai*), a liquid that is offered to one or more gods.[12] It takes place in several very different

[11] See fig. 81a. On this detail, see also J. L. Durand, *Sacrifice et labour en Grèce ancienne* (Paris-Rome, 1986), figs. 32a, 33, 38, 55, 62b, 63, 66, 72, 79.
[12] See J. Rudhart, *Notions fondamentales de la pensée religieuse et actes constitutifs du culte dans la Grèce classique* (Geneva, 1958), 240–245. For the iconography, see F. Lissarrague, "La Libation: Essai de mise au point," and A. F. Laurens, "La

contexts: it marks the beginning or end of an action (e.g., departure or return) and can be included as a single element in a complex set of rituals (e.g., sacrifice, prayer, dedication). In the context of the symposion the libation is the prologue to the consumption of a krater of mixed wine. Typically the first krater is dedicated to Zeus and the Olympian gods, the second to the Heroes, and the third to Zeus Soter. This sequence forms a unit, summed up in the proverbial expression "the three kraters."[13]

It is worth mentioning the position of Dionysus in this ritual procedure, because as the god of wine he is to some degree the object of the offering, as Tiresias explains in the *Bacchae*:

> When we pour libations
> to the gods, we pour the god of wine himself
> that through his intercession man may win
> the favor of heaven.[14]

Though widely attested in the texts, the customary libation at the symposion almost never appears in the images. The pictorial tradition does not address the libation in this context, reserving it for other settings. So it is all the more striking to find a cup on which a satyr holding a *phiale* (a shallow bowl) and a maenad with an oenochoe stand to either side of a krater as they pour a libation (fig. 12).[15]

The near-religious character of a symposion is strongly emphasized in a famous elegy by Xenophanes, in which the philosopher describes not an ordinary banquet but an ideal gathering where men come together to drink out of respect for the gods:

> Now, at last the floor is swept, and clean are the hands of all the
> guests, and their cups as well; one slave puts plaited wreaths on
> their heads, another offers sweet-smelling perfume in a saucer; the

---

Libation: intégration des dieux dans le rituel humain?" in *Image et rituel en Grèce ancienne*, Recherches et Documents du Centre Thomas More 48 (December 1985): 3–16, 35–39.

[13] Rudhart, *Notions*, 242 and n. 6. On the gods that are invoked, see M. P. Nilsson, "Die Götter des Symposions," I (Lund, 1951), 428–442. See the fragments of a red-figure cup: Athens, Acropolis 434; Beazley, ARV 330/5.

[14] Euripides, *Bacchae*, 284–285, trans. Arrowsmith.

[15] Red-figure cup; Paris, Louvre G459; Beazley, ARV 789/4.

12. Red-figure cup, Euaion painter, ca. 470.

mixing bowl stands full of good cheer; and other wine is ready, which promises never to give out——mellow wine in jars, redolent of its bouquet; and in the midst the frankincense sends forth its sacred fragrance; and there is water, cool and fresh and pure. The yellow loaves lie ready at hand, and a lordly table groans with the weight of cheese and luscious honey; an altar in the middle is banked all round with flowers, and singing and dancing and bounty pervade the house. But men of good cheer should first of all praise the gods with pious stories and pure words; they should pour libations and pray for power to do the right (for that is the duty closer to hand); it is no sin to drink as much as you can hold and still get home without an attendant, unless you be very old. Praise that man who even in his cups can show forth goodly thoughts, according as memory serves him and his zeal for virtue is at full stretch. In no wise is it good to relate the fights of Titans and Giants nor of Centaurs, the fictions of men aforetime, or their violent factions, in which there is nought that is wholesome; but it is good ever to have regard for the gods.[16]

This long fragment, quoted by Athenaeus, is essentially programmatic. Xenophanes explains the rules for a proper banquet, stressing first the physical cleanliness of the location and the guests,

[16] Xenophanes *ap.* Athenaeus 11.462c–f (= fr. B1 West), trans. Gulick.

which is a sign of their moral purity. In the center of the space the altar and the krater are in place, linking prayers and libations. Proceeding to the matter of the symposion—the use of language in prepared speeches or poems recited from memory—Xenophanes rejects all the themes of archaic poetry, precisely those that serve as the basis for contemporary Attic iconography.

Thus the elegy sung at the banquet defines an ideal situation; this poem's normative intent is clear and has its visual equivalent on the vases that show drinkers gathered around a krater. These pictures are not always exemplary and propound no philosophical or moral message. Their reflective function, however, is evident, as they mirror the drinkers' behavior. In so doing, they deal with all the aspects, including those attacked by Xenophanes. We see drinkers off-balance, reeling and staggering next to a krater (fig. 13);[17] likewise, a long frieze shows how the wedding feast of Pirithoos degenerates into a violent brawl between Lapiths and Centaurs (fig. 14).[18] All the implements are misused: cushions, torches, and skewers become weapons; a table is smashed. The communal krater is present on the left, set upon a tripod, but the wine has stopped flowing. These scenes are like the profane stories Xenophanes would not permit to be sung at the symposion, yet they often appear in painting as counterexamples to the model of the harmonious banquet.

The krater holds an important place in the pictorial vocabulary, not only as a stable point among the drinkers' couches but also in motion, when the guests make their way to the symposion. On a red-figure *pelike*, a flute player leads the procession and is followed by a young man carrying a krater, from the foot of which a flute case hangs (fig. 15).[19] The two youths are garlanded, as is the krater; this highlights both the festive quality of the scene and the importance

[17] Red-figure cup; Karlsruhe, 70/395; J. Thimme, *Griechische Vasen, eine Auswahl aus den Sammlungen des badischen Landesmuseums* (Karlsruhe, 1975), figs. 37–39.
[18] Red-figure krater; New York, 07.286.84; Beazley, ARV 613/1. For other brawls, see the red-figure cups: London, E71; Beazley, ARV 372/29; and Leningrad, 651; Beazley, ARV 325/77.
[19] Red-figure pelike: London, E351; Beazley, ARV 570/56.

13. Red-figure cup, detail, ca. 490.

of the vase used for mixing, which is dressed up like a guest. Wine and music are intimately linked in this scene of solemn procession.

Other processions are far livelier (fig. 16).[20] Five youths cavort in every direction around various vases for wine; the two at either end accompany themselves with castanets that put rhythm into their steps; on the ground are an oenochoe and a large drinking cup (*skyphos*) identical to that being carried by the central figure, whose movement is quite disjointed. Although the light, portable vases remain on the ground, one of the dancers hoists a huge volute-krater in his arms. It is as if the natural order of things were temporarily reversed when these young men dance together and play with the crockery.

Such a procession can precede or follow the symposion and, as we can see, it can take many forms, from the most solemn to the most riotously playful. The Greek word for the movement of a group with dancing, music, and wine is *komos*.[21] The term appears on a pitcher that shows four youths wearing wreaths and gesturing

---

[20] Red-figure cup: Paris, Louvre G71; Beazley, ARV 89/21.
[21] On the iconography of the komos, see A. Greifenhagen, *Eine attische schwarz-figurige Vasengatung und die Darstellung des Komos im VI Jahrhundert* (Königsberg, 1929); P. Giron-Bistagne, *Recherches sur les acteurs dans la Grèce antique* (Paris, 1976), 207–297.

14. Red-figure krater, painter of the Woolley satyrs, ca. 460.

15. Red-figure pelike, Leningrad painter, ca. 470.

16. Red-figure cup, Euergides painter, ca. 510.

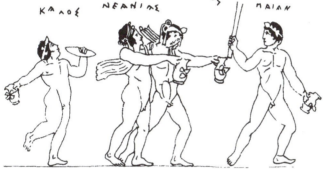

17. Red-figure oenochoe, group of Boston 10.190, ca. 410.

as they walk forward (fig. 17).[22] They are holding small wine jugs (also wreathed) like those given to children on the festival day of the Pitchers, when the storage jars of new wine are opened.[23] This procession is described by the word "komos" written above the inscription *kalos neanias* (handsome youth) and *paian* (paean), a hymn in honor of the gods. "Komos" is the root of the verb *komazein*, "to stage a feast" (see fig. 104), and of the noun *komastes*, "a reveler." One painter borrowed the name Philokomos ("the party goer") for one of his drinkers,[24] and in other paintings we find the label *komarchos*, "master of the revels" (fig. 18).

[22] Red-figure oenochoe: Berlin, 2658; Beazley, ARV 1318/1.
[23] For the feast of the *Choes* (Pitchers), see L. Deubner, *Attische Feste* (Berlin, 1932), 93–122. On this type of vase, see G. Van Hoorn, *Choes and Anthesteria* (Leyden, 1951).
[24] Red-figure cup: Berlin, 2265; Beazley, ARV 88/4. On this name, see Beazley,

18. Red-figure cup, Euergides painter, ca. 510.

The krater has a place of honor in such a komos, transported with gaiety or reverence by the assembled guests. It can also be—and is most often found—set on the ground, functioning as it does in a symposion as the focal point for the visual space.

So it is on a red-figure vase (fig. 19):[25] in the center of the picture, a beardless youth holding a skyphos approaches the mixing vase with his left hand extended toward the liquid. Across from him a bearded man holds a lyre above the krater; obviously he is not about to drop it in. The two figures are making representative gestures that indicate the importance of both the lyre and the krater. The image is a sort of collage that conjoins wine and music, the symposion's essential elements. To the right there are two dancers; one is bearded and carries a drinking horn, while the other is beardless and holds a wineskin. These two objects connote pure wine, as

ARV 1606. *Komarchos*: red-figure amphora: Munich, 2307; Beazley, ARV 26/1. Red-figure cup: Rome, Villa Giulia; Beazley, ARV 173/5.
[25] Red-figure cup: Munich, 2619A; Beazley, ARV 146/2.

19. Red-figure cup, Epeleios painter, ca. 510.

opposed to the mixture symbolized by the krater. To the left stand three men. One is disrobing, while the central figure stretches his hand toward his companion's thigh. This is a scene of homosexual seduction that celebrates the beauty of young men, which is emphasized even more strongly by the inscriptions scattered throughout the background. We find a series of names followed by the epithet *kalos*, "(X) is beautiful." The names are not necessarily those of the figures portrayed, since we find them on other vases in different contexts (see fig. 25). They are plaudits addressed to the handsomest youths, the ones most sought after in Athens at a given time.[26] However, the label "kalos" that appears on a large number of vases expresses verbally what the image shows visually: the aesthetic pleasure derived from looking at a body.

The Athenian erotic world has a twofold character. In the vase paintings we find many youths whose idealized beauty wins the admiration of spectators and guests. They attend the banquets, like the handsome Alcibiades who comes to recline next to Socrates in Plato's *Symposium*. We also see pictures of women whose status is difficult to define (see fig. 9); the texts reveal that they are never wives, but rather women whose services are hired: *hetairai* (courte-

[26] For a list of these names, see Beazley, ABV 664–678; ARV 1559–1616; *Para* 505–508. See also K. J. Dover, *Greek Homosexuality* (Cambridge, Mass., 1978).

sans), musicians, or just companions for the evening who join in the pleasures of the krater.

Within this set of images, everything takes place as if the krater created a hospitable space defined by the sharing and distribution of wine. As we have seen, the process of mixing is only rarely depicted. Most attention is paid to the assembly of drinkers around the communal bowl, whether they be reclining on their couches or engaged in dancing. The krater is like a fixed focus for the activities of the guests, both at rest and in motion. So the container in which mixing occurs becomes the privileged symbol of hospitality; imagery can push this concept to its logical extreme and keep only the vase to denote the whole of the banquet. In the tondo of a cup in the Louvre we see a young slave, a *pais*, dip an oenochoe into a garlanded krater; he is holding a cup in the other hand and is about to serve drinks (fig. 20).[27] By isolating this detail, the painter implies all the aspects of a symposion shown in other, more complicated images. The tondo, however, is not a simple excerpt from a whole that the viewer's visual memory can easily fill in; it is an elliptical portrayal of all the possible forms of conviviality centered on a krater.

Another tondo confirms this analysis:[28] a krater is set to the left, but there is no practical gesture to make it work as a utilitarian object (fig. 21). Alongside it stands a lyre-player with his mouth open, singing in the way Pindar describes: "The voice grows bold next to the krater."[29]

The singer accompanies himself on the lyre, from which a flute-case is hung. Three musical modes—song, lyre, *aulos*—are linked to the concept of wine, as if to sketch the whole scale of the poetic performances that can take place in a symposion.

Yet another variation:[30] a lyre-player stands between a krater and a low statue, formed of a rectangular pillar that is topped by a male head and furnished with an erect phallus (fig. 22). This is a

[27] Red-figure cup: Paris, Louvre G133; Beazley, ARV 348/7.
[28] Red-figure cup: Paris, Louvre G127; Beazley, ARV 427/1.
[29] Pindar, *Nemean*, 9.49.
[30] Red-figure cup: Paris, Louvre G245; Beazley, ARV 366/86.

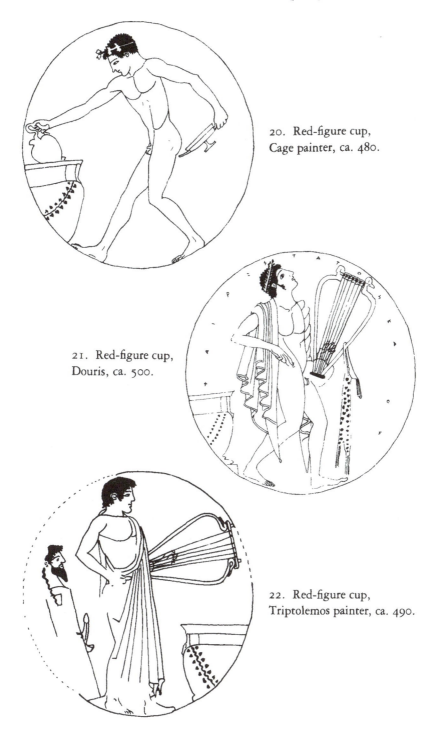

20. Red-figure cup,
Cage painter, ca. 480.

21. Red-figure cup,
Douris, ca. 500.

22. Red-figure cup,
Triptolemos painter, ca. 490.

herm, a signpost at entryways and crossroads that marks the sectors
of the city's public space. The conjunction of this signpost and the
krater shows how the vase for mixing wine can itself become a land-
mark, at once fixed and movable, that allows for the construction of
a changeable sense of space. By now it is clear that the image of the
krater goes well beyond the realistic representation of an object necessary to the Greeks for proper drinking.

The language of poetry confirms this conclusion in its meto-
nymic substitution of the word "krater" for the word "symposion,"
as in Theognis: "We have many companions around the krater, but
few when matters get serious."[31]

The krater, therefore, is imbued with symbolic significance.
It is the symbol of hospitality; it is linked with music and dance; it
is the source for the distribution and circulation of wine; and it
structures the space both of the symposion and, in a more complex
way, of visual imagery.

The world of men finds its parallel around Dionysus in the
world of satyrs. These two levels sometimes overlap, as we have
seen, and the painters like to contrast them or compare them in
many different ways. There is a good example of such imaginative
play on the rim of a black-figure *dinos* (fig. 23).[32] The image does
not occupy the body of the vase, the cylindrical surface, but rather
its upper part, an unbroken circle around the mouth of the krater.
It is a long frieze of little figures dancing and gesturing, a komos
that encircles the liquid contents of the vase. The only static figure
is the seated Dionysus, who is holding a rhyton. In front of him,
Hermes is presenting the god Hephaistos, who is riding on a mule.
On both sides of Dionysus, maenads dance with satyrs, who carry
branches or drinking cups. Half the entourage is made up of satyrs
with horses' tails, but—toward the top of the circle—there are more
numerous male figures who have no tail. These are no longer satyrs
but plain humans. They too carry vases, and a few of them are accompanied by dogs. It is worth noting that their dance is organized
around a krater placed on the ground; pictorially it is almost directly

[31] Theognis, 643–644; see 981.
[32] Black figure: Würzburg, HA166a; CVA I (39), pl. 44.

36

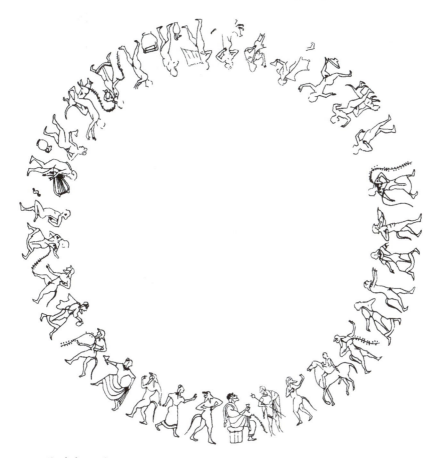

23. Red-figure krater, ca. 520.

across from Dionysus and seems to be correlated to him. Here, in human space, the krater plays the same role as Dionysus does among the satyrs: it is the pole, the axial center for their dance and the source of their celebration.

Dionysus is the master of wine, the only one who can drink without danger. But the god's human form leads the painters to put him into the realm of human gestures. To indicate his great power, they associate him with the krater, not because he drinks from it but because it is still the symbol of the conviviality and happiness of the symposion over which he presides. Thus we find satyrs surrounding him as he reclines at a banquet, resting on a cushion in a most hu-

24. Red-figure amphora, Berlin painter, ca. 490.

man manner.[33] A flute-playing satyr provides the musical accompaniment (fig. 24, top), while on the other side another satyr draws a drink from the krater (fig. 24, bottom). In a striking break with tradition, however, the cup bearer is not standing upright; he is creeping toward the krater, and there is no guarantee that he will hand out the wine without trying to keep some for himself (see also fig. 20).

In another painting a satyr is emptying the contents of a wineskin into a garlanded krater;[34] no water is in evidence (fig. 25). Several inscriptions explain what is happening. In front of the satyr's

[33] Red-figure amphora: Paris, Louvre G201; Beazley, ARV 201/63.
[34] Red-figure cup: Munich, 2619A; Beazley, ARV 146/2. For the exterior of this cup, see fig. 19.

25. Red-figure cup, Epeleios painter, ca. 510.

open mouth is the phrase *hedus oinos* ("wine is sweet"), and above his head *silanos terpon*, which can either be his name ("the silenus Terpon") or, more suggestively, a caption, because *terpon* can be a participle—"a Silenus enjoying himself."[35] The other inscription, along the satyr's back—*kalos epeleios* ("Epeleios is beautiful")—is fairly trite and has no direct connection to the picture (see fig. 19). As we have seen, this kind of remark alludes to eroticism in a homosexual sphere, and this eroticism is reflected by the satyr's shameless erection. Once again wine and eroticism are linked, but now with the excess appropriate to the satyr's world.

The same is true of an amazing komos in which five satyrs cavort wildly to the music of a flute (fig. 26).[36] Two of them are walking on their hands, with their rear ends in the air, symbolizing

[35] Compare this with London, E65; Beazley, ARV 370/13. See also the satyr *Terpaulos* on a red-figure amphora from Berlin (1966.19 = Beazley, *Para* 323/3, twice [cf. fig.96]); and another, *Terpekelos*, on a black-figure aryballos: New York, 26.49; Beazley, ABV 83/4.

[36] Red-figure cup: Brussels, A723; Beazley, ARV 317/15.

26. Red-figure cup, proto-Panaitian group, ca. 490.

their upside-down world; the one on the left is seen full-face, and his stare reaches out to the viewer.[37] In the middle another satyr is riding a huge bird, not airborne but walking; the satyr is leaning on a staff and guiding the bird with some reins. In place of a head this rare bird has a phallus, and so is a startling hybrid steed for the hybrid companion of Dionysus. In the god's imaginary entourage, sexual desire takes the form of an ornithological joke.[38]

Out of all the festive processions led by Dionysus, there is one that is both extraordinary and representative, that is, the return of Hephaistos to Mount Olympus. The scene appears frequently on Attic vases; there are almost 130 examples. On one of them, the

[37] On this point, see F. Frontisi-Ducroux, "In the Mirror of the Mask," in C. Bérard et al., *A City of Images*, trans. D. Lyons (Princeton, N.J., 1989), 151–165.

[38] On this type of winged creature, see A. Greifenhagen, *WZRostock* 16 (1967): 451; W. Arrowsmith, "Aristophanes' *Birds*: The Fantasy Politics of Eros," *Arion* (1973), esp. 164–167, on the pun *eros/pteros*; and J. Henderson, *The Maculate Muse* (New Haven, 1975), 128. See also fig. 68.

27. Red-figure oenochoe, Eretria painter, ca. 420.

procession is led by a flute-playing satyr, while a young beardless satyr guides the mule carrying Dionysus and Hephaistos (fig. 27).[39] The names of the two gods are given in an inscription, along with the word *"komos"*; here the latter has to be the satyr's "stage name," and it is especially appropriate for this scene.[40]

One of the mythical traditions about Hephaistos says that he was born lame, and that Hera in fury hurled him off Mt. Olympus. To get revenge Hephaistos crafted a golden throne, on which Hera sat and found herself trapped. When she could not be freed, the gods called Hephaistos back to Olympus. Dionysus went to fetch him, and, to overcome his resistance, got him drunk. This set of images celebrates both the return of a god under the influence of wine and the triumph of Dionysus.

A krater attributed to the Kleophrades painter strikingly

[39] Red-figure oenochoe: New York, 08.258.22; Beazley, ARV 1249/12.
[40] The name *komos* is often used for satyrs; see V. Fraenkel, *Satyr- und Bakchenna-men auf Vasenbilder* (Halle, 1912).

41

highlights the connection between the two deities.[41] On one side Hephaistos is riding on a mule led by a satyr; another satyr follows behind, playing a cithara. On the other side, Dionysus strides on foot, holding a cithara and a branch of a grapevine; he is preceded by a flute-playing satyr and followed by one playing the *barbiton*, a sort of oblong lyre.

The variety of instruments seems to suggest that this world is suffused with music, in an astonishing combination of styles equaled only by the diversity of the utensils carried by the satyrs marching next to the handles. On one side, there are three satyrs (fig. 28 top). The one on the left has an ivy-wreathed amphora on his shoulder. The one on the right carries an enormous volute-krater; his face is turned outward, like a mask, toward the viewer, whom the satyr seems to address with a wave of his hand, as if to invite him into the procession.[42] The two vases, the amphora and the krater, complement one another; here the krater symbolizes the hospitality of the symposion that has been occasioned by Hephaistos's wrath. Between the two satyrs with wine, the third one is carrying a set of tools, like mallets, that belong to the smithy of Hephaistos, who himself is carrying an axe. All the implements serve to recall the god's technical prowess; he works with molten metal and knows how to invent all sorts of magical devices, beginning with the throne for Hera. The two sets of objects—the artisan's tools and the vase for the symposion—align two technologies, those of iron and of wine. Since wine is often compared to fire,[43] the painter is actually evoking parallel technologies and, through them, two kinds of cunning intelligence (*metis*):[44] Hephaistos tricked Hera, and Dionysus overcame Hephaistos.

This interpretation is confirmed by the activity of the four satyrs next to the opposite handle (fig. 28 bottom). Although the

[41] Red-figure krater: Harvard, 1960.236; Beazley, ARV 185/31. Compare this with the red-figure pelike—Paris, Louvre G162; Beazley, ARV 186/47—which shows Hera fastened to the throne.

[42] Cf. n. 37, and compare the red-figure pelike, Paris, Louvre G227; Beazley, ARV 283/2.

[43] Eratosthenes of Cyrene *ap*. Athenaeus, 2.36ff.

[44] See M. Detienne and J.-P. Vernant, *Cunning Intelligence in Greek Culture and Society*, trans. J. Lloyd (Atlantic Highlands, N.J., 1978).

28a & b. Red-figure krater, Kleophrades painter, ca. 500.

image is fragmentary, we can see clearly that the two central satyrs
are dancing, flanked by two others. The outer one on the left is
carrying a skin full of pure wine, while the one on the right is not
only playing the flute but is also burdened with a massive leather
bellows; its tube is hanging in front of his thigh, and its wooden
handle is visible next to the knee of the neighboring satyr. Once
again the symposion and the forge are brought into correspondence
through these objects, which are typologically similar, visually anal-

43

ogous, and even sometimes denoted by the same Greek word, *as-kos*.[45] Similarly the bellows tube and the flute are both called *aulos*,[46] creating another link among the disparate skills of metallurgy, music, and the use of wine.

In his playful depiction of this set of instruments and utensils, the painter was able to turn the riotous parade into a concrete manifestation of the power of Dionysus. Hephaistos, cast down from Olympus, could not remain in exile, and his acceptance back into the company of the gods took place through the komos led by Dionysus. Hephaistos was ensnared by drinking too much wine, but the presence of the krater in this procession serves as a reminder of the importance of hospitality, even among the gods.[47]

The krater is the material sign of the apportionment of wine, and it allows for control over the amount and intensity of the wine that is consumed. In a lost comedy by Euboulos, Dionysus himself explains:

> For sensible men I prepare only three kraters: one for health (which they drink first), the second for love and pleasure, and the third for sleep; after the last one is drained, those who are deemed judicious go home. The fourth krater is not mine any more—it's for insolence; the fifth is for shouting; the sixth is for rude banter; the seventh is for fistfights; the eighth is for disorderly conduct; the ninth is for ill humor; and the tenth is for madness, and that one knocks you out. When it's poured neat into a small jar, it easily trips up the one who's drunk it.[48]

But there is more. As a symbol of mixing and sharing, set in the middle of the guests, the krater serves as a focus for space and

---

[45] See H. Blümner, *Technologie und Terminologie der Gewerbe und Künste bei Griechen und Römern* (Leipzig, 1879), vol 2.191.

[46] See LSJ s.v. *aulos*. The bellows appears in other paintings. For example, red-figure cups: Paris, Cabinet des Médailles 542 and 539; Beazley, ARV 483/133 and 134; a red-figure krater: Vienna, 985; Beazley, ARV 591/20; and a fragment from a red-figure stamnos: J. Paul Getty Museum, 76.AE.151.26.

[47] Cf. the red-figure kraters: Bologna, Pell. 303; Beazley, ARV 1184/6; Adolphseck, 77; Beazley, 1346/1.

[48] Euboulos *ap*. Athenaeus, 2.36b (= fr. 94 Kock).

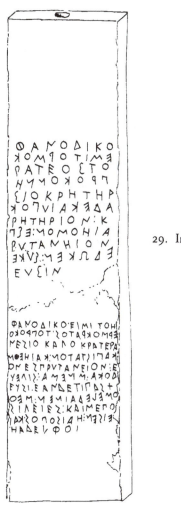

29. Inscription from Sigeum, ca. 550–540.

embodies all the values of the mean, *meson*.[49] Both stable and mobile, it binds together the komos and the symposion, the two occasions of wine-centered conviviality, and it permits the creation of a changeable environment. As the vessel shared by all the drinkers and the source for the distribution of wine, it is established in the middle of the egalitarian group of guests.

[49] For the symbolic content of *meson*, see N. Loraux, "Solon au milieu de la lice," in *Hommage à H. von Effenterre* (Paris, 1984), esp. 201.

45

Thus the krater becomes a privileged, honored object, a unique symbol for everything the symposion means to Greek culture. It is a luxury item, often crafted of precious metal—bronze, silver, or gold[50]—and thus belongs among the *agalmata*, the offerings particularly dear to the gods.[51] For one final example we may consider a krater mentioned in an inscription from Sigeum in Asia Minor (fig. 29).[52] Dating from the mid-sixth century B.C., the inscription is carved in the archaic *boustrophedon* (ox-turning) style, running from left to right and then back again like the furrow in a plowed field. The text is repeated twice, with some variations, first in Ionic dialect and then in Attic; it states that one Phanodikos has donated a krater, along with its filter and stand (see fig. 10). It is a splendid offering as a civic dedication, set up in the *prytaneion,* the city hall where public banquets are held; it shows the bond that unites the donor and his fellow citizens and their equality in the sharing of wine.[53] The symposion is often actually and metaphorically a political occasion; in the *Banquet of the Seven Sages* Mnesiphilos of Athens, friend and admirer of Solon, observes: "In my opinion, Periander, conversation, like wine, should not follow the rules of plutocracy or aristocracy; rather, like democracy, it should be equally shared among all and belong to them in common."[54]

[50] We may recall the famous kraters of Vix or Derveni. See C. Rolley, *Les Bronzes grecs* (Fribourg, 1983), figs. 129, 158, 159.

[51] On this term, see L. Gernet, "The Mythical Idea of Value in Greece," in *The Anthropology of Ancient Greece*, trans. J. Hamilton and B. Nagy (Baltimore, 1981), esp. 101–105. Numerous kraters appear in temple inventories, as for example in Delos (*ID*, no. 104). See Herodotus, 1.25, 51.

[52] Today it is in London at the British Museum. For a transcription of the inscription, see Dittenberger, *Sylloge* 3, no. 2; see also the commentary by M. Guarducci in G.M.A. Richter, *Archaic Gravestones of Attica* (London, 1961), 165–168. The double text can be translated as follows: "I am from Phanodikos, son of Timokrates of Prokonesos; he has given a krater, a pedestal and a strainer to the prytaneion at Sigeum. / I am from Phanodikos, son of Timokrates of Prokonesos; I too have given a krater, a pedestal and a strainer as a memorial, to the prytaneion at Sigeum. If something happens to me, O Sigeans, take care of me. Aesop and his brothers made me."

[53] On the *prytaneion*, see S. Miller, *The Prytaneion* (Berkeley-Los Angeles, 1978), and P. Schmitt-Pantel, *La Cité au banquet*, chap. 2.

[54] Plutarch, *Banquet of the Seven Sages*, 11.154c.

Chapter 3

Manipulations

"We do not attend a banquet like vases to be filled, but to speak seriously and to jest, to hear and to deliver the speeches that the occasion requires of the participants, if they are to take pleasure from conversing among themselves." The foregoing remarks are made by Thales in the *Banquet of the Seven Sages*.[1] The guests are not merely passive consumers; at a symposion it is not enough just to drink wine, and the vases are not simply practical objects. The mixture of water and wine is complemented by a mingling of all possible pleasures: visual, olfactory, and acoustic. The symposion is defined by its variety and its ludic qualities: games of skill and balance, flights of fancy and feats of memory, verbal jokes, which are not the sole property of buffoons (like Philippos in Xenophon's *Symposium*) or of comic poets (like Plato's Aristophanes).[2] There is much play in the creation of all that allows for the transition from one level to another. The symposion could be defined as a locus for metaphor and illusion, both poetic and visual. Many of these games have wine—which is not just a beverage—as their point of departure, in addition to the vases, which become toys or bodies that are handled and, in turn, manipulate the drinker.

Greek potters shared their workshops with artisans in terra-

[1] Plutarch, *Banquet of the Seven Sages*, 2.147e.
[2] Xenophon, *Symposium*, 1.11; Plato, *Symposium*, 189–193.

30. Corinthian plastic vase, ca. 580.

31. Corinthian plastic vase, cross section.

cotta, and there are many similarities between pottery and small-scale modeling in clay; sometimes the two genres are linked and give rise to "molded vases," which have a very long tradition.[3] The artisans' skill enabled them to create complex objects, whose function goes well beyond that of a drinking cup; these are small sculptures, delicate and often badly preserved.

Some of them hold surprises for the user, like a piece made in Corinth that consists of a squatting fat man and a krater

[3] See M. I. Maximova, *Les Vases plastiques dans l'Antiquité* (Paris, 1927).

(fig. 30).[4] The portly drinker wears a panther skin on his back, and although he has sometimes been called a satyr, he is neither grotesque nor bestial. Only his obesity is abnormal. His posture, with his arms extended toward a vase decorated with a frieze of horsemen, is also unusual, as if he were ready to drink the contents of the vase. He is like someone parched by thirst and eager to quench it, without any intention of sharing with others as is customary at a symposion. The bottom of the krater has a hole that empties into the statue's base, which takes the form of a hollow circular crown; the drinker himself is hollow and also opens into the base, so that his body and the krater are connected; the same action fills both the vase and the stomach of the statuette (fig. 31). The seated figurine has small holes in his back and the top of his head to let air out as liquid rises within his body. Tilting the whole piece backward sends the entire contents of the vase into the drinker's body; if the two air holes are then plugged, the liquid stays hidden and the krater empty. When the holes are opened, air pressure pushes the liquid back into the vase, which looks as if it were filling itself automatically. This amusing fact of physics makes the object dynamic. It recalls the miracles attributed to Dionysus, like the fountains of wine or miraculous kraters, like the one at Elis which Pausanias describes with a certain amount of skepticism:

> The worship of Dionysus is one of the principal Elean cults, and they say the god himself visits them at the feast of Thuia. They hold the feast they call Thuia about a mile away from the city. The priests take three empty basins in the presence of the citizens and of any foreigners there may be and deposit them in a building. The priests themselves, and anyone else who wants, put seals on the doors of the building; the seals can be inspected the next day, and then when they go inside they find the basins full of wine. The most distinguished men in Elis and foreigners as well have sworn that this happens as I have said, though I myself was not there at the moment of the feast. The Andrians say that every second year on the feast of Dionysus their sanctuary runs with wine of its own

[4] Paris, Louvre CA454; CVA 8 (12), pl. 4 (501). See E. Pottier, "Le Satyre buveur," in *Recueil Pottier* (Paris, 1937), 220–231; H. Payne, *Necrocorinthia* (1931), 175–176. Another "automatic" vase is described by Achilles Tatius, 2.3.2.

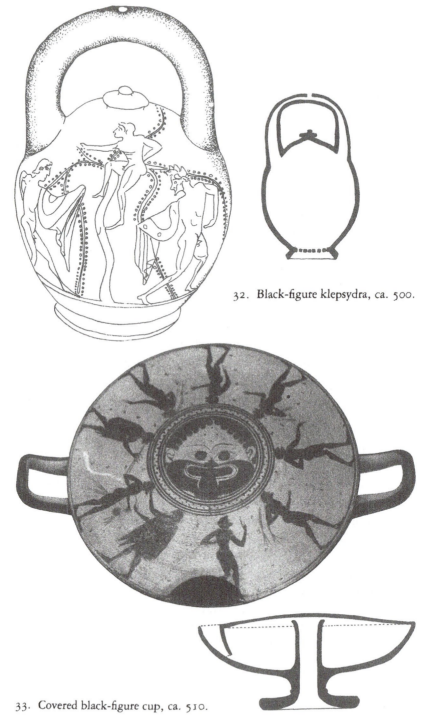

32. Black-figure klepsydra, ca. 500.

33. Covered black-figure cup, ca. 510.

accord. If these Greek stories are to be believed, then by the same reckoning one should accept what the Aethiopians above Syene say about the table of the sun.[5]

No matter how skeptical Pausanias may be, we should be careful not to mistrust Dionysus here.

Other vases show how skillfully the potters used certain elementary principles of physics regarding vacuum and pressure. A fragment of a poem by the fifth-century philosopher Empedocles compares breathing to the movement of air and water in a *klepsydra* (water clock) being swung by a little girl;[6] he is referring to a closed vase whose base is riddled with small holes; the handle consists of a hollow tube that forms an arc over the vase and has a small opening that can be covered by one's thumb (fig. 32).[7] When the vase is submerged in a liquid and the opening in the handle is uncovered, the vase fills up as air escapes. If this opening is then stopped up, the liquid can be transported and will not run out through the strainer in the bottom until the opening is cleared again. Thus a slight movement of the thumb can control the liquid's rate of flow. This vase is a kind of watering can, and although it was probably *not used in connection with the drinking of wine*, it does demonstrate the hydraulic expertise of the Athenian craftsmen.

Such skill is also manifested in other kinds of vases that do belong to the symposion. First, there are the covered cups, which have a fixed lid covering the entire bowl except for a small crescent that just allows for the contents to be placed to one's lips. The lid can be decorated in a variety of ways, either in a circular pattern or as a tondo. Encircling a *gorgoneion*, for example, we find a group of athletes accompanied by a flute player in procession toward the one who is crowning the victor (fig. 33).[8] Such a vase cannot be filled in

[5] Pausanias, 6.26, trans. Peter Levi, Penguin ed.

[6] Empedocles *ap.* Aristotle *Resp.* 7 (= fr. 100 DK, fr. 551 Bollack); see J. Bollack, *Empédocle 3. Les origines, commentaire 2* (Paris, 1969), 474–478.

[7] Baltimore, Robinson; CVA 3 (7), pl. 3 (297)1, and text pp. 12–13. Cf. the red-figure cup, Florence, 91288; CVA 4 (38) pl. 134 (1706)1; Beazley, ARV 891/2, *Para* 429. See also W. Deonna, "Vases à surprise et vases à puiser le vin," *Bulletin de l'Institut Genevois* 38 (1908): 3–29.

[8] Black-figure cup, Boston, 95.16, unattributed. On this type of cup, see Caskey-Beazley, *Attic Vase Paintings in the* MFA, *Boston* 1 (Oxford, 1931), 33–34. For

the usual manner from the top; inside it has a hollow base that extends almost even with the lid. When this cup is lowered into a krater, it is filled through the base, and when it is removed from the liquid and set level, it can be emptied only through the crescent from which one drinks. The contents cannot be seen, nor can they be spilled if they are shaken during the act of drinking. The reveler does not have to stay thirsty.

Other vases have a hollow base that can be filled with a very small amount of liquid, and once again a small hole lets one control the liquid's movement within this hidden reservoir. If one opens the hole while passing the cup to a companion, he gets soaked. The "dribble glass" is not a modern invention![9] Sometimes the hollow base contains small terracotta balls, so that the cup sounds like a rattle when it is shaken;[10] the drinking vessel becomes a musical instrument.

The potters also knew how to make vases with double walls to keep wine cool. Thus an amphora can be made of two containers nested one within the other; double openings, at the neck and near the base, allow the outer part (which is not accessible through the mouth of the vase) to be emptied (fig. 34). The wine in the inner vessel can be chilled by filling the outer layer with ice water. The existence of such a cooling-amphora (*psykter*) shows the degree of elegance attained by the Athenian symposion by the second half of the sixth century B.C.[11]

Boeotian examples, cf. Oxford, 1929.656; CVA 2 (9), pl. 52 (416)12, and p. 109; Paris, Louvre CA797; CVA 17 (26), pl. 46 (1169) 5, and p. 48.

[9] See J. Noble, "Some Trick Greek Vases," *PAPhS* 112 (1968): 371–378, esp. fig. 4; and M. Vickers, "A Dirty Trick Vase," *AJA* 79 (1975): 282, pl. 50.

[10] See M. Vickers, "A Note on a Rattling Cup," *JHS* 90 (1970): 199–201, pls. 4–5; M. Vickers, "An Ex-Rattling Cup," *AJA* 77 (1973): 196–197 and 364; M. Vickers and L. Jeffrey, "Two More Rattling Cups," *AJA* 78 (1974): 420–431, pl. 88.

[11] Black-figure psykter-amphora; Boston, 00.331; Beazley, *ABV* 307/62; CVA 1 (14), pl. 33 (655), fig. 28 and p. 25, where there is a list of known examples. To these should be added a red-figure psykter-krater recently acquired by the Metropolitan Museum of Art in New York (1968.11.12, attributed to the Troilos painter); see Christie's London, July 1986, no. 141, p. 38.

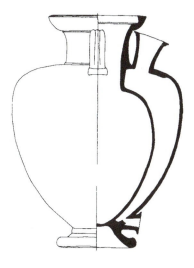

34. Black-figure amphora-psykter, outline and cross section, ca. 530.

The virtuosity of the potters in the Kerameikos also found expression in a totally different area: not just in cooling vases or trick cups, but in people or animals combined with vases. We find a satyr crouching on an amphora and clinging to its handles, as if on a skittish mount (fig. 35); he is in the same position as the satyr riding a phallus bird (see fig. 26). On his back rests a drinking cup decorated with a mythological scene, which shows Hermes next to a palm tree during the quarrel between Heracles and Apollo over the Delphic tripod.[12] It is not clear if such a hybrid object should be called a vase or a statuette. The satyr's amphora is no longer a vase but a vehicle, and the statue becomes the prop for a vase; the drinker might be surprised at the double function of such a piece, which is both a drinking cup—which can be lifted by its vertical handle— and also a comic illustration of one of the ways satyrs use vases.[13]

There is a comparable, though regrettably fragmentary, statuette that seems to have consisted of a donkey whose load was attached to its back by two large cinches (fig. 36).[14] Its cargo is actu-

[12] Sarajevo, 654; CVA I (4), pl. 27 (154). On the quarrel between Apollo and Heracles, see D. von Bothmer, "The Struggle for the Tripod," in *Festschrift für F. Brommer* (Mayence, 1977), 51–63.

[13] See chap. 4, p. 000, and figs. 63–66.

[14] Agrigento, inv. S65; Beazley, ARV 29/2. The reverse has traces of a reclining

35. Plastic vase, ca. 510.

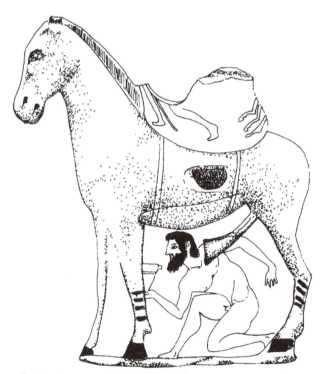

36. Plastic vase, style of Euthymides, ca. 510.

ally the neck of a drinking cup, part of whose decoration survives: a banqueter, a crouching man, men's legs, and the hooves of a ram. Under the donkey's belly, on a platform that connects its legs, is a kneeling drinker who is raising a drinking cup. The donkey, the exemplary Dionysiac animal, becomes part of a striking visual and figurative game: his cargo becomes a functional object, a drinking cup; the figure between his hooves recalls the motion of the komos. A set of metaphorical shifts, from the cargo to the cup, from the statuette to the self-portrait of the drinker, creates the illusion and the double meaning characteristic of such an object. There is a complete blending of two levels: the aesthetic (the imitation of reality) and the functional (the prop for a drinking vessel).

Without pushing the analogy too far, we might recall Alcibiades' famous eulogy of Socrates in Plato's *Symposium*:

> I shall praise Socrates in a figure (*di'eikonôn*) which shall appear to him to be a caricature, and yet I do not mean to laugh at him but only to speak the truth. I say then, that he is exactly like the masks of Silenus, which may be seen sitting in the statuaries' shops, having pipes and flutes in their mouths; and they are made to open in the middle, and there are images of gods inside them.[15]

The object Alcibiades mentions, a kind of case in the shape of a Silenus, is not exactly like the things we have found, but it does belong to the same category of small artisanal sculpture. It also yields a similar double meaning, an illusion, a surface appearance that we must go beyond. The Socratic illusion opens into philosophical truth. Our figured vases are not so loftily ambitious: beneath the visual meaning of the sculpted and painted shape, the truth of these little vases lies in the wine they hold.[16]

---

figure (Dionysus?) and a crouching man; between the donkey's hooves is another crouching man.

[15] Plato, *Symposium*, 215a, trans. Jowett.

[16] Cf. London, E785, unattributed; CVA 4 (5), pl. 37 (230) 1. There are several such vases by Sotades or in his style, Beazley, ARV 764/8–11; 765/1; 766/2–4 twice; 768/30–31. Above all there is the extraordinary collection now in the J. Paul Getty Museum, Malibu, Calif., particularly the red-figure kantharos 85.AE.363. These vases have been studied by M. True, *Pre-Sotadean Attic Red-*

37. Black-figure cup, manner of the Lysippides painter, ca. 520.

The artists also played less complex games with another feature of the vases, in making them into bodies. Just as we speak of
vases in anatomical terms—neck, belly, shoulder, foot, lip—the
Greeks spoke of a vase's "ears" (*ota*, its handles), head (*kephale*), face
(*prosopon*), and lips (*cheile*); the *phialai* for libations have a navel (*om-
phalos*).[17] These anatomical details are sometimes transformed into
physical realities. There are several vases in the form of a foot, or of
sexual organs (fig. 37);[18] the base of a cup might be replaced by a
phallus.[19] It then becomes difficult to call such an object a mere
vessel. Its practical function is subsumed by the anatomical illusion
it engenders, and in bringing it to his mouth the drinker is explicitly drawn into an erotic game. Since a picture is worth a thousand
words, my argument will get enough confirmation from a painted

---

figure Statuette Vases and Related Vases with Relief Decoration (Ph.D. diss., Harvard,
1986).

[17] *Kephalot*: Aristophanes, *Plutus*, 545; Alcaeus *ap*. Athenaeus, 10.430d (= fr.
Z22 Lobel-Page). *Prosopon*: Athenaeus, 11.501d. On this point, see W. Froehner,
Anatomie des vases antiques (Paris, 1876), and J. Boardman, "A Curious Eye-Cup,"
AA (1976): 281–290.

[18] See J. Ducat, *Les Vases plastiques rhodiens* (Paris, 1966), 146ff. An example from
Boston (13.105; Beazley, ABV 170/1) belongs to the potter Priapos; see Boardman, "A Curious Eye-Cup," 289, n. 28. See also A. Pasquier, "Deux objets la-
coniens méconnus au Musée du Louvre," BCH 106 (1982): 281–306.

[19] Black-figure cup; Oxford, 1974.344, published by Boardman, in "A Curious
Eye-Cup," who gives a list of similar vases, p. 287. Add a red-figure cup; coll.
D. J. Stähler, *Eine Sammlung griechischer Vasen* (Münster, 1983), no. 15, pl. 20.
See also the odd red-figure stamnos; Ferrara, T128 VT, unattributed; S. Auri-
genna, *La Necropoli di Spina in Valle Treba* (Rome, 1960), p. 46ff., pl. 37.

38. Red-figure cup, ca. 510.

cup that shows such a vase being handled by a nude woman in the position of a banqueter (fig. 38).[20]

The play of metaphors is used in all its ramifications; just as the body is a vase, the vase is a body. The analogy between drinker and vase also extends in another direction. The vase with sexual organs attached is decorated with eyes, between which stands the mask of a satyr with pointed ears (see fig. 37). Such a frontal view is not uncommon in the realm of images (see figs. 25, 27), and—in its direct address to the viewer's gaze—it creates a sense of fascination that is one of the features of the Dionysiac world.[21] On this vase the effect is heightened even more by the presence of a pair of eyes flanking the satyr; they turn the back of the cup into a mask covering the drinker's face. Thus the vase is simultaneously a receptor of and a charm against the evil eye.

The exploration of the anatomical potentials of a vase goes even farther. There exists an important set of molded vases in the form of heads, human or animal. From the animal kingdom examples are gathered from the whole zoological spectrum, both wild and domesticated, known to the Greeks: lion, eagle, stag, wild boar,

[20] Red-figure cup: New York, 56.171.61; Beazley, ARV 50/192. Cf. ARV 450/22.
[21] See F. Frontisi-Ducroux and J.-P. Vernant, "Figures du masque en Grèce ancienne," in J.-P. Vernant and P. Vidal-Naquet, *Mythe et tragédie deux* (Paris, 1986), 25–43.

39. Red-figure kantharos, ca. 440.   40. White-ground kantharos, ca. 480.

dog, and donkey.[22] On the human side the choices seem to have some meaning. They are never true portraits but generic types, and there are no gods except for Dionysus and Heracles; instead one finds only women, both male and female blacks, Asians, and satyrs. These vases are most often of a single head (fig. 39),[23] or of two joined back-to-back in a study of contrasts, such as white woman/black woman (fig. 40).[24] There is just one type that does not exist: the "ordinary" white male. It is as if the anthropology of such molded vases was meant to define the opposite of the Greek drinker and to hold up to him all the things that he was not. As was noted above, the experience of wine is also the experience of the Other; this set of vases seems to conform to such an outlook, and it sums up the view

[22] H. Hoffmann, *Attic Red-figured Rhyta* (Mayence, 1962).
[23] Red-figure kantharos; Naples, H 2948; Beazley, ARV 1547/4.
[24] White-ground kantharos; Boston, 98.926; Beazley, ARV 1534/9. The whole set is reorganized by Beazley, ARV 1529–1552 and *Para* 501–505.

41. Red-figure cup, Oltos, ca. 510.

attributed to Thales: "He often used to say that he had three reasons to be grateful to the gods: 'First, because by birth I am human and not a beast; second, because I am a man and not a woman; finally, because I am a Greek and not a foreigner.' "[25] This kind of anthropology that proceeds by serial exclusion is typically Greek.[26] At the symposion we find it embodied in the drinking cup on the table; the encounter between drinker and vase generates meaning.

The interactive game between drinker and vase also functions in the dialogue created by the custom of writing on the vase. We have already commented on some of the inscriptions that accompany the painted scene. Though sometimes unrelated to the figures, like the *kalos* praises (see fig. 19) or the artists' signatures (see fig. 9), they are more often directly connected as identifications or captions (see figs. 18, 25, 27). Occasionally they are the words being spoken by the people depicted (see fig. 21).[27]

Two nude women are reclining on pillows (fig. 41).[28] One of them is playing a flute, and to her right the other one holds a beaker

[25] Thales *ap*. Diogenes Laertius, 1.33 (= fr. 11 A1 DK).
[26] See P. Vidal-Naquet, *The Black Hunter*, trans. A. Szegedy-Maszak (Baltimore, 1986), 1–12.
[27] See F. Lissarrague, "Paroles d'images: remarques sur le fonctionnement de l'écriture dans l'imagerie attique," in *Ecritures II*, ed. A. M. Christin (Paris, 1985), 71–95.
[28] Red-figure cup; Madrid, 11 267; Beazley, ARV 58/53.

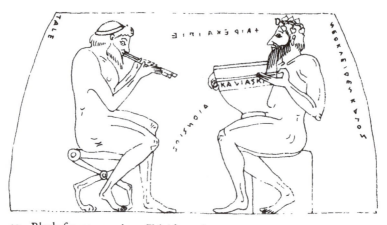

42. Black-figure oenochoe, Taleides painter, ca. 550.

and proffers a *kylix* to her companion. Running right to left, in the same direction as the drinker's gesture, is the inscription *pine kai su*: "You drink too." The text explains the movement in the image; it is an invitation that goes along with the passing of the cup; the wine is passed around, as it should be, and conversation follows.

There is a similar invitation on a black-figure vase that shows two bearded men sitting side by side (fig. 42).[29] To the left is a flute player and across from him is an ivy-crowned man holding a large krater, who is identified by a slanted inscription as "Dionysios"; this is not the god, but a man with a theophoric name. Two vertical inscriptions run along the side of the picture: on the left is the beginning of a signature, *tale{ides epoiesen}*, "Taleides made me"; on the right is the erotic salute *neokleides kalos*, "Neokleides is beautiful." Between the two faces, again from right to left, is the exhortation *khaire kai pie*, "Be of good cheer and drink."

The latter can be interpreted in one of two ways, depending on the level of reading that is assumed to govern it. As on the previous cup, it could be a remark addressed by the drinker to the flute player, and thus it would be within the level of the painting itself. On the other hand, if we see it as being on the surface of the vase as such and not as part of the scene, it would become a standard in-

---

[29] Black-figure oenochoe; Berlin, inv. 31 131; Beazley, ABV 176/2.

43. Black-figure cup, Nikosthenes potter, ca. 530.

scription, like the signature or the praise. It would no longer be "intra-iconic" but reach from the vase to the person holding it. Since the inscription runs from one face toward the other, it leads one to think that it records conversation. Nonetheless the painter is clearly aware that his vase is a medium for writing as well as for imagery; on the vase held by the drinking figure is the beginning of the inscription *kalias ka{los}*, "Kallias is beautiful." On this vase, then, we find both a marginal inscription outside the image—*neokleides kalos*—and an inscription of the same type—*kalias kalos*—integrated into the scene. Image and text coexist in a very sophisticated relationship, which crosses easily from one level to another.

My uncertainty about the status of the inscription *khaire kai pie* does not stem from a wish to complicate matters, but from the fact that there is an overlap between the two alternatives—an utterance within the image, or a label on the vase. The second formula, a remark conveyed from the vase to the person using it, is the more common (fig. 43).[30] Beneath a scene showing two lions devouring a bull, fitting the archaic comparison that epic poetry uses to denote the valor of a hero, we find the legend *khaire kai piei tende*, "Be of good cheer and drink me" (fig. 44).[31] The demonstrative pronoun *tende* is in the first person and refers to the vase, the one issuing the invitation. The verbs are second-person singular imperatives and re-

[30] Black-figure cup; Rome, Vatican 456; Beazley, ABV 235.
[31] Black-figure cup: Limassol (1961), 298, fig. 49. For the epic simile, see *Iliad* 15.323–325, and A. Schnapp-Gourbeillon, *Lion, héros, masques* (Paris, 1981), 39–48. For this type of motif, see K. Schauenburg, "Zu attischen Kleinmeisterschalen," AA (1974): 207.

44. Black-figure cup, ca. 550.

fer to the drinker. Such linguistic markers create a conversational situation, in which the interlocutors are the drinker and his cup.[32]

Such formulas also occur on the cups ascribed to "little masters," in the second half of the sixth century. These are quite elegant, with the rim marked off from the bowl by a black line (fig. 45).[33] In the upper border the decoration is kept to a minimum: one or two animals, an individual or even a simple bust. The lower portion contains a line of writing, with the letters regularly spaced, to greet the drinker or identify the potter. The text clearly has ornamental value and functions like a decoration; indeed, in some cases the vase carries only writing, as on a cup inscribed *su khaire kai piei*, "You, be of good cheer and drink" (fig. 46).[34] The exhortation is made stronger by the pronoun *su*, "you," at the beginning of the sentence; with the image gone, the text stands by itself.

The formulas in such inscriptions have an interesting variety.

[32] E. Benveniste, "L' Appareil formel de l'énonciation," in *Problèmes de linguistique générale* 2 (Paris, 1974), 79–88.

[33] Black-figure cup; Brussels, R386; CVA 1, pl. 2 (15), 4. On these cups, see the articles by Beazley: "Little-Master Cups," JHS 52 (1932): 167–204, especially 194–195 for the inscriptions; "Two Inscriptions on Attic Vases," CR 57 (1943): 102–103; "Ten Inscribed Vases," *Eph. Arch.* 1 (1953–54): 201–202.

[34] Basel, market; M.u.M. *Auktion* 60, no. 18.

45. Black-figure cup, ca. 550.

46. Lip cup, ca. 550.

We often find the verb *khaire*, which is usually translated as "be of good cheer" but is also the most general form of greeting. It is suitable for the symposion, whose goal is pleasure and enjoyment, and it is the word Theognis uses to express his delight:

> I take pleasure in drinking well (*khairo d'eu pinon*)
> and in singing to the notes of the flute.
> I also delight in holding the harmonious lyre in my hands.[35]

Theognis's formulation is repeated almost word for word on a cup where we find *khaire kai piei eu*, "Be of good cheer and drink

[35] Theognis, 533–534.

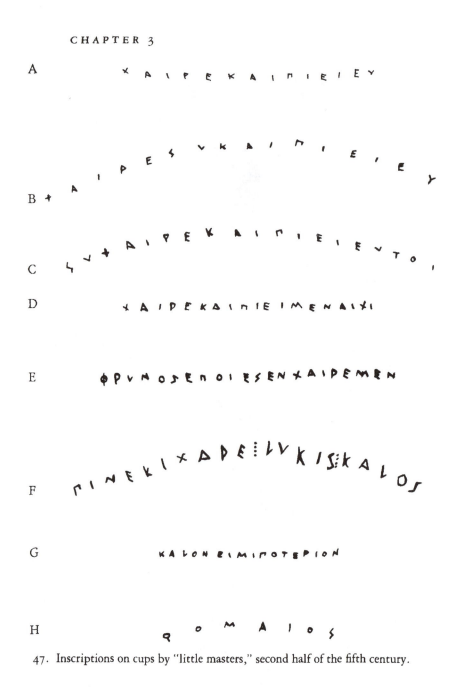

A ΧΑΙΡΕΚΑΙΠΙΕΙΕΥ

B +ΑΙΡΕΣΥΚΑΙΠΙΕΙΕΥ

C ΣΥ+ΑΙΡΕΚΑΙΠΙΕΙΕΥΤΟΙ

D ΧΑΙΡΕΚΑΙΠΙΕΙΜΕΝΑΙΧΙ

E ΦΡΥΝΟΣΕΠΟΙΕΣΕΝΧΑΙΡΕΜΕΝ

F ΠΙΝΕΚΙΧΑΡΕΙΛΥΚΙΣΚΑΛΟΣ

G ΚΑΛΟΝΕΙΜΙΠΟΤΕΡΙΟΝ

H ϘΟΜΑΙΟΣ

47. Inscriptions on cups by "little masters," second half of the fifth century.

well" (fig. 47A).[36] The use of the adverb *eu*, "well," is worth noting; in English "have a good drink" and "drink well" are not synonymous. The Greek comprises both senses and moreover has a distinct moral connotation, to drink moderately and without excess. Once again we find the concerns of Xenophanes and the advice given by Dionysus in the comedy by Euboulos.[37]

Other versions emphasize the recipient, *su* (fig. 47B, C), or the sender, the cup, that speaks in the first person, *me* (fig. 47D). On some vases the painters combine different types of inscription: for example, the signature of the potter Phrynos (fig. 47E), followed by a greeting, or by an invitation to drink and erotic praise (fig. 47F).[38] In one case the adjective *kalos* even applies to the vase itself: *kalon eimi poterion*, "I am a beautiful drinking cup" (fig. 47G).[39] Another cup, also unique, has the simple adjective *komaios*, which can be understood either as a term descriptive of use—"a vase for a revel"—or as an epithet, rare but not unknown, of Apollo Komaios (fig. 47H).[40]

The verbal game between vase and drinker puts the vase into action and makes it function in its context, the symposion. It can happen that the painter chooses to locate himself in another context, prior to the history of the vase. When on a cup garlanded with ivy we find *khaire kai prio men*, "Greetings—buy me," we are still in the potter's workshop, as customers;[41] still, the ivy crown already hints at the vase's future employment (fig. 48).

[36] Fig. 47a: Christchurch, 1/53; Beazley, *Para* 78/1 twice; CVA, New Zealand, 1, pl. 27, 3–4. Parallels are too numerous to be mentioned here; see K. Schauenburg, "Herakles und Bellerophon," *Med. Ned. Inst. Rom* 6 (1979): 9, and n. 1.
[37] See chap. 2, notes 16 and 48.
[38] Fig. 47b: Tübingen, H/10.1222, unattributed; CVA 3 (47), pl. 27 (2272), and pp. 38–39. Fig. 47c: Berlin, F1769; Beazley, *Para* 75. Fig. 47d–e: London, B424; Beazley, ABV 168. Fig. 47f: Leningrad, 210 (St 216), B1412; Beazley, ABV 669.
[39] Fig. 47g: Rhodes, 10 527; Beazley, ABV 162/1. The same formula occurs on London, B601.7; Beazley, ABV 79. Paris, Louvre F66; Beazley, JHS 52 (1932): 178, n. 21. Medellin (Badajoz); M. Almagro Gorbea, *XI Congr. Nac. Arq.* (Merida, 1969), 437–448.
[40] Fig. 47h: Würzburg, H5036; CVA 1 (39), pl. 40 (1922), 3–4, p. 45.
[41] Oxford, 1965.120; Beazley, ABV 57/112. For this formula, see the articles by Beazley: JHS 52 (1932): 182; AJA (1935) 476; AJA (1950) 315–316. See also R. Blatter, *AA* (1973): 67–72; *AA* (1975): 350–351.

48. Siana cup, ca. 550.

49. Fragment of a red-figure krater, Kleophrades painter, ca. 500.

This kind of inscription has many and varied modes of expression. The painters knew how to make full use of such abundance, opening the way for a long tradition of "speaking vases." As a final example we may consider an exceptional instance of graphic refinement—in the two senses of the verb *graphein*, which means both "to write" and "to draw."[42] On a fragment of a krater, next to a flute player, stands a drinker whose only surviving trace is the cup he is holding, which has the inscription *{kh}aire*, "be of good cheer" (fig. 49). Here the cup's message to its owner is sent from the krater that underlies the image out to the actual guests. It is an image *en abîme*, and it operates, as a true visual and verbal sign, both in the figural space on the surface of the cup and in the real space of the symposion around the krater.

[42] Red-figure krater: Copenhagen, inv. 13 365; Beazley, ARV 185/32.

Chapter 4

Drinking Games

In their imaginative relation to games, the Greeks go well beyond the efforts we have just observed. In addition to the interplay between the inscription, the vase on which it appears and its intended receiver, the interplay between molded form and painted decoration, and the surprises concealed within the interior of a vase, we find a set of games that takes place not just *on* the objects but *with* them. Removing the implements associated with wine from their ordinary role, the symposion uses them for various exercises in skill and balance.

THE WINESKIN AS A TOY

The wineskin, *askos*, is made of soft leather, a goatskin turned inside out whose texture is sometimes suggested by painted marks (see fig. 25). In Euripides' *Cyclops*, the skin is the miraculous container that holds the wine with which Odysseus will trap his opponent. The Cyclops is a monstrous cannibal who devours Odysseus's companions; unaware of culture and of the gifts of Dionysus, he is familiar only with cups containing milk. Plotting to blind him, Odysseus introduces him to wine without explaining its use, and eventually the Cyclops staggers in, happily drunk, having made the acquaintance of Dionysus:

CYCLOPS: Mamama. Am I crammed with wine!
How I love the fun of a feast!
The hold of my little dory
is stuffed right up to the gunwales!
This marvelous meal reminds me:
I should go feast in the soft spring
with my brothers, the Cyclopes.
Here, here, my friend, hand me the flask. . . .

ODYSSEUS: Listen, Cyclops. I've spent a lot of time with this
drink of Bacchus I gave you.

CYCLOPS: What sort of god is this Bacchus held to be?

ODYSSEUS: Best of all in blessing the lives of men.

CYCLOPS: At least he makes a very tasty belching.

ODYSSEUS: That's the kind of god he is: hurts no one.

CYCLOPS: How can a god bear to live in a flask?

ODYSSEUS: Wherever you put him, he's quite content.

CYCLOPS: Gods shouldn't shut themselves up in wineskins.

ODYSSEUS: What matter, if you like him? Does the flask irk you?

CYCLOPS: I loathe the flask. The wine is what I like.[1]

Dionysus is amusingly incarnated; the wineskin becomes the skin of the god. In his honor, on the second day of the Dionysia, the Greeks celebrated the Askolia by hopping onto a wineskin, as the ancient commentators tell us.[2] The verb *askoliazo* can have two different etymologies; if connected to *skele* (leg), it means "to limp" or "to hobble along," and this is the explanation we use today. Since antiquity, however, the verb has also been linked to *askos* (wineskin), and this popular etymology must have occasioned the use of the wineskin in this game, which is doubly difficult: the player has to keep his balance on a leather object that has been inflated until it is round and made slick with grease.[3]

---

[1] Euripides, *Cyclops*, 503–510, 519–529, trans. Arrowsmith.
[2] Suidas, s.v. *askos*; scholia to Aristophanes, *Plutus* 1129.
[3] Plato, *Symposium*, 190d; Suetonius, *Des Jeux Grecs* 12, ed. J. Taillardat (Paris, 1967), 71, and commentary, pp. 170–171; W. Deonna, *Un divertissement de table: à cloche pied* (coll. Latomus 40, Brussels, 1959); K. Latte, "Askoliasmos," *Hermes* 85 (1957): 385–391. In the Luxembourg Gardens in Paris, near the Medici fountain, there is a modern incarnation of this game crafted in bronze by E. L. Lequesne in 1851.

50. Red-figure cup, Euergides painter, ca. 510.

Several vases depict exercises of this kind. In the tondo of a fragmentary cup (fig. 50), a young man is crouching on a sizable wineskin while struggling to maintain his position.[4] Sometimes the player sits astride the skin, as does an ephebe, who is also using a drinking horn like a trumpet (fig. 51, left).[5] This parodies the departure for battle, as the container for pure wine now serves as a mount for the knight sounding the call to arms, and the parody is complemented on the other side, where a real warrior, armed with a shield, blows an actual trumpet (fig. 51, right). Joined on the surface of the same cup, these two images exemplify the game that is always possible between the outside world and the realm of the symposion.

Another cup shows even more complicated activity (fig. 52).[6] Eight youths, almost all garlanded across the chest, are exercising in two groups of four. An ephebe is stretched out on the ground and supports two of his companions; one is propped on the prone man's

[4] Red-figure cup: Tübingen, E41; Beazley, ARV 94/104.

[5] Red-figure cup: Paris, Louvre G70; Beazley, ARV 169/6; see also Beazley, ARV 14/3, 49/178, 125/13.

[6] Red-figure cup: Basel, BS463; Beazley, ARV 147/16. For balancing acts, see the black-figure cup: Leningrad St., 46, unattributed. See also the red-figure cup: Brussels, A3047; Beazley, ARV 146/7.

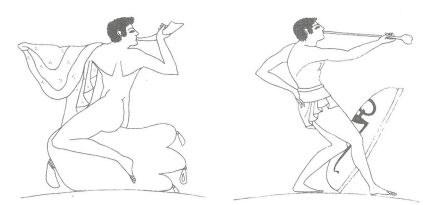

51. Red-figure cup, Scheurleer painter, ca. 510.

52. Red-figure cup, Epeleios painter, ca. 510.

knee while the other rests his right hand on the latter's head. These two face each other and lean backward, thereby creating not exactly a human pyramid but a scaffolding of bodies in tension and equilibrium. The fourth moves toward them, perhaps to take his place in the structure. To the right, two other youths cavort around a rudimentary chariot, which is being pulled by a third. Tied to the chariot's shaft is a wineskin on which the last ephebe tries to keep his place, not by straddling it but by balancing himself. These two exercises, vigorous as they are, seem to require both strength and grace; taken as a whole, the image privileges a sort of collective ephebic prowess, as part of a komos that proceeds on the other side of the vase around a krater placed on the ground.

Such examples make it clear that what is involved is an expression of skill and of balance. The game using the wineskin, *askoliasmos*, generates a kind of displacement; it is no longer the wine itself that disorients and dizzies the drinker, but the container for the wine. To avoid falling, the player has to use all his skill in controlling the elasticity, the shape and the slippery surface of the object under him; in so doing, he maintains his own security, *asphaleia*. The game puts into practice an important attribute of the god in whose honor it is played, for Dionysus is the one who sets upright (*orthos*), as Philochoros explains:

> Amphictyon, king of Athens, learned from Dionysus the art of mixing and was the first to make such a mixture: so it is that men began to stay upright while drinking, whereas in earlier times the pure wine had left them prostrate; therefore he erected an altar for Dionysus the upstanding (*orthos*), in the sanctuary of the seasons.[7]

Dionysus, however, is also the one who makes men stagger, who keeps them from walking straight or standing up, who knocks their feet out from under them—he is Dionysus Sphaleotas or Sphaltes, "the one who trips you."[8] The game of *askoliasmos* that elicits all the frenzied energy of the youthful drinkers is a worthy homage to Dionysus, master of wine both pure and mixed, master of balance and stability—and collapse.

Satyrs of course deal with lots of wineskins, and the askos seems to be one of their favorite accessories. It can substitute for the pillow on which the drinker reclines, as in a picture showing a satyr with one skin hung at his feet, while another serves as his cushion (fig. 53);[9] he is singing, playing the castanets, and has his leg flexed as if he were about to leap up.

[7] Philochoros *ap.* Athenaeus 2.38 c–d (= FGrHist 328 F 5b Jacoby).
[8] See M. Detienne, *Dionysus at Large*, trans. A. Goldhammer (Cambridge, Mass., 1989), 46–50.
[9] Red-figure kantharos: New York, 12.234.5; Beazley, ARV 382/183. On this detail, see Caskey-Beazley, *Attic Vase Paintings in the* MFA, *Boston* 1 (Oxford, 1931), 29; also, J. Moebius, *AA* (1964), cols. 294–300.

53. Red-figure kantharos, Brygos painter, ca. 480.

54. Red-figure cup, ca. 500.

Elsewhere some satyrs juggle a set of wineskins that seem to be very light, as if inflated with air (fig. 54).[10] The Greeks used the proverbial expression "to be terrified by an askos" to describe someone who is needlessly afraid.[11] Other satyrs use wineskins as floats to sail on the ocean's waves in a kind of maritime komos, where they can be expected to pitch and sway (fig. 55).[12]

[10] Red-figure cup: Würzburg, L471; Beazley, ARV 129/20.
[11] Suidas, s.v. *askos: askoi mormoluttesthai.*
[12] Red-figure cup: Paris, Louvre G92; Beazley, ARV 134/3. The askos does float, but it does not sink if the oracle given to Theseus is to be believed (Plut. *Theseus* 24.5–6). On the sea-borne komos, see chap. 6, pp. 115–117.

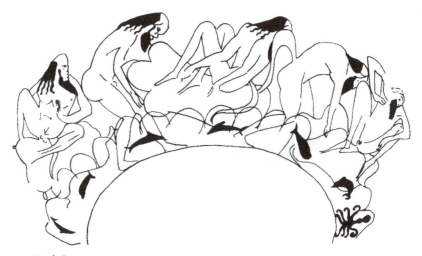

55. Red-figure cup, ca. 500.

Back on land, we find a satyr riding a wineskin and trying to pass a kantharos under his arm without spilling it (fig. 56).[13] It is a double test of balance; with the satyr on the skin and the cup in his hand, the exercise becomes all the more risky—satyrs always overdo it.

On another cup, two satyrs ride their wineskins in pursuit of one carrying a krater (fig. 57, top);[14] on the other side, a maenad clad in a panther skin blows a trumpet, giving the signal for two chariots to spring forward (fig. 57, bottom). The teams are odd, not horses but more maenads and satyrs, with satyrs as drivers. The trumpet sounds the alert . . . for the guests; the equipment for the contest—a wineskin, a basket of provisions, a dead hare—brings us back to the world of the symposion. The image blends warfare and reveling, and it transforms satyrs into warriors of wine. Oh, what a lovely war! Another satyr is similarly placed between two formats

[13] Red-figure cup: Brussels, A723; Beazley, ARV 317/15 (the exterior of this cup is shown here as fig. 26). See the red-figure cups: Boston, 95.34; Beazley, ARV 75/64; Baltimore, Robinson; Beazley, ARV 316/7.

[14] Red-figure cup: Cambridge, 37/17; Beazley, ARV 133/4. For another use of the askos, attached to the satyrs' backs, see a black-figure Ionian dinos: Würzburg, H5352; CVA I (39), pl. 26. See also a painted cloth from Gela: D. Adamesteanu, "Coppi con teste dipinte da Gela," *Arch. Class.* 5 (1953): 1–3.

56. Red-figure cup,
proto-Panaitian group, ca. 490.

57a & b. Red-figure cup, wider circle of the Nikosthenes painter, ca. 510.

75

58. Red-figure alabastron, Berlin painter 2268, ca. 500.

(fig. 58).[15] He is brandishing a wineskin, and an amphora lies at his feet, but at the same time he is carrying a curved shield decorated with a protective eye; this is the light armor of the peltasts, who fight from ambush.[16] The blood that flows when satyrs go to war looks enough like wine to be mistaken for it.

BALANCING ACTS

The drinkers' skill is not limited to games with the wineskin. A large number of images show different exercises of various types that involve all parts of the body. On a cup attributed to Epictetos, a drinker sits on the ground, with his body turned forward in a rather ungainly position (fig. 59).[17] On his extended left arm a cup is balanced in the crook of his elbow. In his right hand he holds a pitcher, perhaps—although we cannot be sure—with the aim of pouring its contents into the cup. Still, it is clear that the exercise

[15] Red-figure alabastron: Providence, 25.073; Beazley, ARV 157/88. Cf. the red-figure cup: London, E3; Beazley, ARV 70/3; and F. Lissarrague, "Dionysos s'en va-t-en guerre," in *Images et société*, ed. C. Bérard (Lausanne, 1987), 111–120.
[16] See F. Lissarrague, *L'Autre Guerrier: archers, peltastes, cavaliers dans l'imagerie attique* (forthcoming).
[17] Red-figure cup: Oberlin, 67.61; Beazley, *Para* 329/14 twice.

59. Red-figure cup, Epiktetos, ca. 510.

consists of defying gravity and handling the vessels in unfamiliar ways, without the use of one's hands and without holding the handles.

Another cup offers another variation (fig. 60):[18] here the drinker uses his left foot and leg to carry both his cloak (on his shin) and a pointed amphora (on his foot). Flexing his right leg, he maintains his balance with his hands. Ordinary gestures and postures are forgotten, as the body undertakes strange new poses; once again the norm is abandoned.

According to the same principle, all parts of the body other than the hands can be used to hold a vase; that the head too is excluded is not surprising, since women make their way to fountains by carrying water jugs on their heads or shoulders. In contrast a youth attempts to hold his cup in his teeth while keeping his arms and legs extended (fig. 61).[19] Another young reveler uses his belly to carry a huge krater, and he flaunts his excitement as a satyr would (fig. 62).[20]

In this realm, too, satyrs are the unchallenged champions. They can hold vases with a foot (fig. 63), on a back (fig. 64), or—most improbably—on the end of a penis, as on a cup where the satyr

[18] Red-figure cup: Paris, Louvre F129; Beazley, ARV 84/20.
[19] Red-figure cup: Adria, B471; Beazley, ARV 349/2.
[20] Red-figure cup: Paris, Louvre G73; Beazley, ARV 280/24.

60. Red-figure cup, Skythes, ca. 520.   61. Red-figure cup, ca. 480.

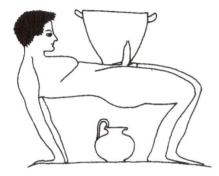

62. Red-figure cup, ca. 510.

has a companion who brandishes what must be an empty amphora and turns its neck toward his phallus (fig. 65).[21] The satyrs' drunkenness matches their sexual voracity; treated as bodies, the vases can be erotic partners too. If we had any doubt about the satyr's intention, we would only have to look at a section from an amphora in the Louvre to understand the meaning of the satyr's gesture (fig.

[21] Fig. 63: red-figure pelike: Tübingen, E54; Beazley, ARV 280/24. Fig. 64: red-figure cup: Berlin, 2267; Beazley, ARV 111/16. Fig. 65: red-figure cup: Boston, 01.8024; Beazley, ARV 173/9; see also the red-figure psykter: London, E768; Beazley, ARV 446/262.

63. Red-figure pelike,
Flying Angel painter, ca. 480.

64. Red-figure cup, Hermaios painter,
signed Khakhrylion, ca. 500.

65. Red-figure cup, Ambrosios painter, ca. 500.

66. Red-figure amphora, Euthymides, ca. 520.

66).[22] There are many ways to get satisfaction: the vase can be a sexual partner, just as it can be a steed (see fig. 35). Alongside the game of balance is a game of substitution between vase and body; the two satyrs are like a visual equivalent for the old Greek pun *pinein/binein* (to drink/to fuck).[23] "No Aphrodite without Dionysus," says the proverb.[24]

In the world of the satyrs, the drinking vessel plays its part as an instrument of pleasure.

THE WINE OF LOVE

The game most frequently associated with the symposion, the one to which Athenaeus devotes half a book and which often appears in the images, is the game of *kottabos*.[25] The texts do not tell us as

[22] Red-figure amphora: Paris, Louvre Cp 11072; Beazley, ARV 27/7. On this gesture, see F. Lissarrague, "The Sexual Life of Satyrs," in *Before Sexuality*, ed. D. Halperin, J. Winkler, and F. Zeitlin (Princeton, N.J., 1990), 53–81.
[23] See Aristophanes, *Frogs*, 740.
[24] *Corpus Paroemiographorum Graecorum* II, pp. 320–321, Leutsch-Schneidewin. Aristophanes calls wine "the milk of Aphrodite" (Athenaeus, 10.444d).
[25] On this game, see Athenaeus, 11.487d–e and 15.665c–668f. See also the studies by K. Sartori, "Das Kottabos-Spiel der alten Griechen" (diss., Munich, 1893); B. Sparkes, "Kottabos: An Athenian After Dinner Game," *Archaeology* 13 (1960):

much as we would like. Without being flatly contradictory, they describe a range of activities from which we can extract the essential points.

The game does not consist of drinking but of flinging some wine onto a target. It is more a matter of skill than of balance, since the drinker's success depends on steadiness in aim and action. He has to have a fine sense of touch, as a character in a comedy tells his friend:

A: Pick up the cup and show me how it's done.

B: You have to be like a good flute player and spread your fingers as you bend them; pour out a bit of wine—not too much—and let fly.[26]

The player should also bend his wrist with smoothness and elegance. The painters paid close attention to this detail, and the hands of the players actually resemble those of flute players (see figs. 24, 41).

The game can take many forms, depending on what has been chosen as a target. Sometimes small saucers are floated in a basin of water that is set between the guests; the wine has to hit these tiny boats and sink them. We sometimes see a disk balanced flat on top of a tall pole; when knocked off by the wine, it falls and crashes into a kind of sconce attached to the center of the pole. The latter variant is depicted allusively in several different kinds of images, as on an oenochoe that shows a seated woman taking aim at the target with the cup in her hand, while a youth with a ladle stands by (fig. 67).[27]

We know of another kind of target from a single cup by Apollodoros (fig. 68).[28] It shows some banqueters aiming at a target set

---

202–207; Suetonius, *Des Jeux Grecs*, ed. J. Taillardat (Paris, 1967), commentary pp. 166–167.

[26] Antiphanes *ap.* Athenaeus, 15.667a (= fr. 55, line 15 Kock). The Greek says *Auletikos dei karkinoun tous daktulous* (you must crab up your fingers like a flute player). On the relation between the crab and the flute, see Beazley, ARV 224/1, Karkinos painter.

[27] Red-figure oenochoe: Berlin, F2416; Beazley, ARV 1020/99.

[28] Red-figure cup: private collection; M. Vickers, *Greek Symposia* (London, n.d.), fig. 17, p. 15.

67. Red-figure oenochoe, Phiale painter, ca. 440.

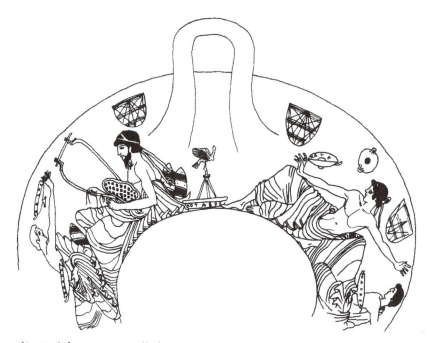

68. Red-figure cup, Apollodoros, ca. 490.

69. Red-figure psykter, Euphronios, ca. 520.

70. Red-figure hydria, Phintias, ca. 520.

under the cup's handle, in the place sometimes occupied by a krater (see fig. 9). The target consists of a flat pan, on which stands a tripod that is balancing a phallus-headed bird. The identity of the game is certain because the pan is inscribed KOTABOS. This target is unique; it is not a simple disk but a phallus-bird, which we have already seen among the satyrs (see fig. 26),[29] and which emphasizes the erotic nature of this game.

While getting ready to throw his drops of wine, the player declares for whom he is playing, and so dedicates his turn to a lover. Thus a reclining nude woman named Smikra (Little One) flings her wine in honor of Leagros (fig. 69): *"Tin tande latasso leagre* (For you, Leagros, I am throwing this {portion})."[30] The Dorian dialect may recall the game's Sicilian origins. Similarly, on a *hydria* two reclin-

[29] See chap. 2 and fig. 26.
[30] Red-figure psykter: Leningrad, 644 (St. 1670); Beazley, ARV 16/15.

71. Red-figure stamnos, Copenhagen painter, ca. 480.

ing women are making the moves of kottabos (fig. 70), and the one on the left has her mouth open to say *"Soi tendi euthumidei* (This is for you, Euthymides).*"*[31]

These two examples make it quite clear that kottabos is more than a game of skill. Whatever form it may take, it involves true aim and the disruption of equilibrium, whether it be of a disk on a pole or of a little saucer floating in water. When the balance is upset, something capsizes or falls with a crash, and this symbolizes that love has been assured. The break in equilibrium is the physical sign of the uncertainty that takes hold of a lover in the presence of the beloved. The game requires an amatory partner, and before the throw one calls out to all the other guests the name of the person being targeted. The gesture always has an intended receiver, and the vases that carry such a person's name are not uncommon.

Dionysus himself takes part in the game on a vase that shows him drinking with Heracles (fig. 71).[32] The god is turning his cup, and running next to his face and along his arm is the remark *toi tende* ("this is for you"). To the left a cup-bearing satyr completes the thought *lykoi* ("for Lykos"), a name that is known from other inscriptions.[33] This is human, all too human, praise; the painter has

[31] Red-figure hydria: Munich, 2421; Beazley, ARV 23/7.
[32] Red-figure stamnos: Paris, Louvre G114; Beazley, ARV 257/14 and 1596.
[33] See Beazley, ARV 1595–1596, and ABV 670.

72. Red-figure cup near
Apollodoros, ca. 490.

made Dionysus the mouthpiece for a drinker of his own day, and has
projected the behavior of men onto the realm of the gods.

Elsewhere the kottabos player is seen frontally, facing the
viewer in a sort of challenge (fig. 72).[34] The inscription *ho pais kalos*
("the youth is beautiful") is not near the face, as if the player were
speaking, but seems to spring from his cup and follow the trajectory
of the wine, as in the line from Alcaeus: "The wine drops are flying
from the Teian cups."[35]

Some features of this game make it similar to divination; it
tries for control over the future and supplies a definite answer—
success or failure—not to a question asked of a god but to an an-
nounced intention. The outcome of the game serves as an omen;
accurate shooting presages amorous success.

Athenaeus compares kottabos with a libation, as if the former
were a secular version of the latter.[36] While it is true that wine is
poured for both, the analogy should not be pushed too far. At the
symposion a libation is the opening ceremony, not a game of skill.
The libation signifies a link between men and gods that is neither

[34] Red-figure cup: Florence, PD248; Beazley, ARV 121/1.
[35] Alcaeus *ap*. Athenaeus, 11.481a (= fr. I1/322 Lobel-Page).
[36] Athenaeus, 10.427 d. See G. Lafaye s.v. "Kottabos" in Daremberg-Saglio *Dict. ant.*, 3.866. On the libation, see chap. 2, n. 12.

called into question nor left in any way to chance or to the performer's expertise; the element of uncertainty in kottabos has no place in a libation. Nonetheless, it is still true that wine can be handled in many ways, whose symbolic values allow for different interpretations. The idea of sharing that is basic to the Greek use of wine can also be seen in the bond that unites men and gods and that may, or may not, join partners in love.

Chapter 5

Reflections

Let us drink. Why wait for the lighting of the lamps?
Night is a hair's breadth away. Take down the ornate goblets
from the shelf, dear friend, for the son of Semele and Zeus.
Give us wine to forget our pains. Mix two parts water, one part
    wine,
and let us empty the dripping cup—urgently.[1]

Like the vases, poems get broken and come to us only in pieces. The above fragment from Alcaeus describes the moment when the drinking begins, with the guests taking up their ornate (*poikilais*) goblets. It would be good if we could understand this term more fully, to know if it is referring to painted vases, like the ones we are discussing, or to metal vases with engraved or enameled decoration.[2] As it is, we will never know. Alcaeus was not writing for archaeologists. The Attic vases are also extolled by Pindar at the beginning of a poem dedicated to Thrasyboulos of Agrigentum:

Thrasyboulos, I send you this batch of cheerful songs
for your dessert. They will charm the company

---

[1] Alcaeus *ap.* Athenaeus, 10.430c–d = fr. Z22 Lobel-Page (trans. Barnstone, modified). See D. Page, *Sappho and Alcaeus* (Oxford, 1979): 307–309.
[2] On this point, see the arguable but suggestive remarks by M. Vickers, "Les Vases peints: image ou mirage," in *Images et céramique grecque* (Rouen, 1983), 29–42.

of your guests; for the fruit of Dionysus
and the cups sent from Athens, they will be a goad [. . .].[3]

Song is inseparable from wine and from drinking cups, the famous Attic vases, but Pindar says no more. We have to accept the fact that the Greek texts are practically mute on the topic of this pottery, however rich and abundant it may be.[4] In contrast, the ancient poets often treat the activities and the accessories of a symposion, in connection with both the joys of wine and the pleasure of song. Banquet poetry delights in self-representation, and although it is not limited to the charms of conviviality, it does give them pride of place. The reflective play within the poems that tell of a symposion while being sung at a symposion is also found on the vases that show the drinkers their own activity. The painters deliberately and imaginatively explore the potentials of this self-reflexive play.

A red-figure cup shows five bearded men reclining in a continuous circle (fig. 73);[5] one side has a flute player and a youth drawing liquid from a krater, and the other shows three drinkers, one of whom is playing a lyre. This scene rests on a surface marked by a triple line, beneath which is a narrow band with several types of vases in black-on-red silhouette. The lower area, with the vases in black on a red ground, reverses the color scheme of the scene in the upper zone, where the figures are in red against a black background. The two surfaces are clearly separated and do not overlap; the upright handles of one kantharos do extend to the foot of one of the drinkers, but they do not intrude into the picture plane reserved for individuals. The two spaces are discrete; aside from the play of color and its visual effect, the function of the two areas is completely different.

In the upper zone, in red figure, there are people who are moving, drinking, and singing; it is a space made up of verbal,

<hr/>

[3] Pindar *ap.* Athenaeus, 11.480c (= fr. 124 Snell). See B. Van Groningen, *Pindare au banquet* (Leyden, 1960), 84–103.

[4] Nonetheless, see the elegy by Critias *ap.* Athenaeus, 1.28b (= fr. 88 B2 DK). See also the account by Strabo, 8.6.23, and the analysis by H. Payne, *Necrocorinthia*, 348–349.

[5] Rome, Vatican; Beazley, ARV 427/2. For this type of structure, see fig. 76.

73. Red-figure cup, Douris, ca. 500.

gestural, and visual exchanges, and the elements of the picture are organized syntactically, in a narrative pattern. In the lower zone, in black figure, there are objects that are static, in a row, side by side; it is a surface that is purely ornamental and organized paratactically. Usually the cups are decorated with a meander ("Greek key"), or with a continuous pattern that is geometric and not representational.[6] By occupying this space, the vases take the place of ornaments and are differentiated from the vases being used in the upper zone by the drinkers; they exist in counterpoint to the objects being handed around and are placed, as if in exergue, to show the whole range of ceramic possibilities. We find here a dozen small vases: four skyphoi, three cups, a kantharos, three pitchers, and one vase with a phallus for a spout. The use of black glaze robs them of their materiality; they are merely shadows. The mimetic value of drawing shades off into the indexical value of objects that are more than vases;

[6] A list of cups with friezes of vases is provided by D. Buitron (Ph.D. diss., New York, 1976), 25, n. 57. To these should be added Aberdeen, Marischal College 748; Beazley, ARV 871/9; and Xanthos, A33/3027; H. Metzger, *Fouilles de Xanthos* 4, no. 358, pl. 80.

74. Red-figure cup,
Pithos painter, ca. 500.

they are signs. The vase, autonomous, shown for its own sake, is charged with significance. It evokes the pleasures of drinking from it, or playing with it, or simply looking at it.

The result of such a play of signs is a tendency toward abstraction. So it is on one tondo where the rapid brush strokes cannot easily be deciphered (fig. 74).[7] A large triangular black shape blocks the middle of the image; it is a drinking horn (*rhyton*; see fig. 19). Behind it a figure is seen from the back; two vertical lines indicate his spine, and two curves his shoulder blades. His leg is bent to the left, with the knee raised. His head is turned toward the right, and his hair falls in black ringlets onto his left shoulder. His eye is visible just above his right shoulder. This drinker has a Scythian cap (see fig. 1).

Such an image is intelligible only if we remember what it is modeled on and if we know its referent. The rapidity of the drawing and the cursory quality of the execution show that the painter had little interest in mimetic accuracy. This is not a realistic image, but a quick sketch of a drinker at a symposion. Its only distinguishing features are the Scythian cap and the drinking horn, the rhyton, which the man is not holding and whose size is completely out of scale; the vase is superimposed on the image. This is a symbol of the Scythian way of drinking wine, which Anacreon mentions only in order to reject:

[7] Red-figure cup: Rhodes, 13 386; Beazley, ARV 139/23.

75. Red-figure cup, ca. 500.

Boy, bring me
a cup, to drink at a gulp;
mix ten measures of water and five of wine,
so that once again and peacefully
I may honor Dionysus.
Let's not fall
into riot and disorder
with our wine, like the Scythians,
but let us drink in moderation
listening to the lovely hymns.[8]

To drink like a Scythian is to drink unmixed wine; the use of the rhyton in exergue recalls the vase that belongs to Dionysus, who alone can drink pure wine safely. The picture also suggests drinking to excess and the intoxication of the person who drinks immoderately.

An analogous effect is produced by the image of a satyr who has dived headfirst into a vat of wine;[9] since he is upside down, only his legs, tail, and genitals are visible (fig. 75). In front of the vat stands the black silhouette of a cup, motionless and undisturbed, that serves as a reminder of proper manners in drinking. The main image, on the other hand, shows neither mixing nor sharing—the satyr wants it all, right now, as is.

Heracles and Dionysus appear again, flanking a kantharos, on

---

[8] Anacreon *ap.* Athenaeus, 10.427a–b (= fr. 11/356 Page).
[9] Red-figure cup: Geneva, 16 908; CVA 1, pl. 9.

76. Red-figure psykter, Kleophrades painter, ca. 500.

a cooling jar whose bowl is divided into two zones (fig. 76).[10] On the upper level, six satyrs crawl around on all fours. On the lower level stand the two half-brothers; both have Zeus as a father, with their mothers being Alcmene and Semele. They face each other and hold their respective iconographic attributes, Heracles with club and bow, Dionysus with kantharos and ivy. The lower register is a frieze of ten vases, nine cups (*skyphoi*), and one kantharos. This last

[10] Red-figure psykter: Compiègne, 1068; Beazley, ARV 188/66.

is placed between Heracles and Dionysus, immediately beneath the one held by the god, as if to replicate its form. The meeting takes place under the sign of wine shared between Dionysus, master of the symposion, and Heracles.[11]

Such friezes of silhouetted vases have formal and decorative effects that are never empty of meaning; if we attend to them, we find that such visual allusions are not unimportant.

The painters are not satisfied with just decorating the vases, and indeed the images sometimes take over. In its blending of pleasures, the symposion does not neglect the visual but makes room for spectacle. Greek culture is often defined as a culture of language, *logos*, and this is certainly true; but the visual aspect is also important for this society that produces statues, frescoes, embroidery, all kinds of sculptures, carvings, and paintings—of which only the smallest part has survived to our time. If Plato condemned images, it was because he had good reason to distrust them.[12]

The Greeks' visual acuity is evident, as it is elsewhere, in a famous scene from Euripides' *Ion*, where a slave describes the preparations for a feast at Delphi. A large tent has been set up:

> First he cast
> above the roof a wing of cloth . . .
> and there were figures woven in design:
> Ouranos . . . Helios . . . black-robed Night.
> The sides Ion draped with tapestries
> also, but of barbarian design.
> There were fine ships which fought with Greeks, and creatures,
> half-man, half-beast, and horsemen chasing deer,
> or lion hunts. And at the entrance, Cecrops,
> his daughters near him, wreathed himself in coils
> of serpents—this is a gift which had been given
> by some Athenian. Then in the center
> he put the golden mixing bowls.[13]

[11] On Heracles and Dionysus at the banquet, see B. Fehr, *Orientalische und griechische Gelage* (Bonn, 1971), 82–83; T. Carpenter, *Dionysian Imagery in Archaic Greek Art* (Oxford, 1986), 177 and n. 83.

[12] On Plato's criticism of imagery, see J.-P. Vernant, "Naissance d'images," in *Religions, histoires, raisons* (Paris, 1979), 105–137.

[13] Euripides, *Ion*, 1158–1166, trans. Willetts.

The spirit of the symposion, organized around the kraters, is enhanced by an extraordinary pictorial environment. Its iconographic program is carefully thought out, deriving its meaning from its relation to events within the tragedy.[14] Here most attention is paid to the tapestries, and the messenger who is describing the setting does not linger over the golden bowls; nonetheless, the importance of the spectacle is amply attested.

The same is true in Aristophanes' *Wasps*, when the son is trying to teach his father, whose sole passion is jury duty, how to behave at a banquet. He has to show restraint and not rush for the wine.

> SON: Recline, and learn how to be a guest in polite society.
> FATHER: How should I recline? Tell me.
> SON: Gracefully . . . Bend your knees like an agile gymnast, and settle onto the cushions. Then praise one of the bronze vases, study the ceiling, admire the wall hangings.[15]

The decoration in the hall where the drinkers are seated attracts their attention. The symposion itself is part of the spectacle; by the end of the fifth century, it is deliberately construed as such, including performances by professional mimes, actors, and dancers. Thus in the symposion described by Xenophon, a Syracusan takes it on himself to entertain the guests by hiring a dancing girl who vaults across a circle of swords, and a pair of dancers who mime the love affair between Ariadne and Dionysus with such realism that the symposion comes to a halt:

> At the end, on seeing them depart as if to go to bed, the bachelors among the guests swore that they would get married as soon as possible, while those who were husbands leaped onto their horses and sped home to their wives.[16]

---

[14] D. J. Mastronarde, "Iconography and Imagery in Euripides' *Ion*," CSCA 8 (1975): 163–176; N. Loraux, *Les Enfants d'Athéna* (Paris, 1981), 197–253. See also P. Schmitt-Pantel, "Le Banquet ambigu d'Ion," in *La Cité au banquet*, 261–280.

[15] Aristophanes, *Wasps*, 1208–1215.

[16] Xenophon, *Symposium*, 9.7.

Socrates, needless to say, quietly strolls off, disapproving of such circus acts. Elsewhere he gently makes his opinion known to the Syracusan, who is jealous of the attraction Socrates exerts through his conversation:

> I cannot conceive what pleasure this [spectacle] can afford. But if the young people were to have a flute accompaniment and dance figures depicting the Graces, the Horae, and the Nymphs, I believe that they would be far less wearied themselves and that the charms of the banquet would be greatly enhanced.[17]

As we can see, Xenophon's Socrates refers to painting to describe the kind of dance he would like to see performed at a symposion. These two forms of art, which both include some kind of imitation (*mimesis*), are kin, and both belong to what we might call the visual culture of the Greeks.

The archaic symposion is an enclosed space, restricted to a small number of guests who form a self-sufficient community of peers.[18] The pleasure of a symposion consists of mingling wine, music, conversation, and entertainment. The latter, however, is not a spectacle brought in from the outside, as it is in Xenophon's *Symposium* or in our modern cabarets. It is exclusively the image created by the guests, and by the decoration both of the room where the banquet is held and—obviously—of the vases that pass from hand to hand.

Of the vases that we have seen being handled by the drinkers, most have been plain. Sometimes the kraters are wreathed with ivy, but they are not painted. We might conclude that they are meant to represent metal vases, although these too would often have had figures in relief, but it is likelier that the painters did not bother to try for complete precision in detail. Rather, they did so quite rarely, and when they did, the results are very interesting.

[17] Xenophon, *Symposium*, 7.5, trans. Todd.
[18] See L. Rossi, "Il simposio greco arcaico e classico come spectacolo a se stesso," in *Atti del VII convegno di studio: Spettacoli conviviali* . . . (Viterbo Maggio, 1983), 41–50. See also the studies by O. Murray: "The Greek Symposion in History," in *Tria Corda, Studies in Honor of A. Momigliano* (Como, 1983), 257–272; "The Symposion as Social Organisation," in *The Greek Renaissance of the Eighth Century* B.C., ed. R. Hägg (Stockholm: 1983), 195–199.

77. Black-figure oenochoe, Kleisophos, ca. 530.

On a black figure vase signed by the painter Kleisophos and the potter Xenokles, an amazing komos unfolds around a krater (fig. 77).[19] The revelers are barely upright. The one on the left drinks while sitting on the ground, and the one next to him, holding a hand to his back, seems to be staggering. Alongside the krater a flute player is standing next to a guest reclining on the ground with his elbow on a pillow. To the far right a guest is carrying another on his back, and the latter, with his legs in the air in a Rabelaisian pose, is in the process of noisily breaking wind. The effects of wine are vividly represented, and we are far from Socratic tranquility. In the center of the image, in the midst of the roistering, stands the krater from which a youth is drawing some wine. This krater is decorated with a horse, carefully incised into the black glaze of the vase; while this is not the technique used in the main image, it does conform to the black-figure convention of having small details incised rather than painted.

Despite the drinkers' cross behavior, it is worth noting the delicacy of this drawing; in addition to the detail of this picture of a picture, and its iconographic meaning—the horse recalls the aris-

[19] Black-figure oenochoe: Athens, 1045; Beazley, ABV 186. See also the black-figure hydria: Basel, M.u.M. *Auktion* 34, no. 122, pl. 31 (now at the J. Paul Getty Museum); and the black-figure amphora: Samos; Beazley, ABV 151/18.

78. Red-figure hydria, Nikoxenos painter, ca. 500.

tocratic class of knights—we should also note the vase that emerges from the top of the krater. It is a cooling vase (*psykter*), containing the mixed water and wine, that is set inside the krater, which is filled with ice water or snow (see figs. 76, 78).[20] The sophistication of such objects, testifying to an elaborate code for drinking, is not incompatible with the crudest bodily functions. The symposion is really an occasion for passing freely from refinement to loutishness, from the heights of wisdom to the depths of folly.

The action is more subdued on a red figure *hydria* that shows two symposiasts reclining on mats on the floor (fig. 78).[21] Loaves of bread, painted in black, lie before them. The bearded drinker on the left seems to be playing kottabos, although his face is turned toward his young companion, who is holding on to a pitcher and a cup. Between the two men is a krater, garlanded with ivy and holding a psykter; it is also decorated with the figure of a running satyr. Here the secondary image recalls Dionysus's imaginary entourage and offers the drinker a model of Dionysiac otherness.

A similar effect occurs on a krater whose body is decorated in a checkerboard pattern that emphasizes its volume (fig. 79).[22] The neck has a painted scene that shows a youth and three reclining drinkers next to a great, centrally located krater; the presence of a

[20] On this kind of object, see S. Drogou, *Der attische Psykter* (Berlin, 1975).

[21] Red-figure hydria: Kassel, coll. P. Dierichs; P. Gercke, *Funde aus der Antike* (Kassel, 1981), no. 56, pp. 107–111.

[22] Red-figure krater: New York market; K. Schauenburg, "Zu einem spätarchaischen Kolonettenkrater in Lugano," NAC 11 (1982): 9–31; Basel, M.u.M. *Auktion* 70, no. 207, pl. 44.

79. Red-figure krater, ca. 510.

tree indicates that the setting is outdoors. On the small krater, some
dots represent writing, and a figure of Dionysus in black silhouette
holds a rhyton and some branches. The god is doubly present among
the drinkers, both as image and as wine. The image is multiplied
still further if we imagine the "real" krater in the middle of a group
of guests. The painting of Dionysus is like a doubling *en abîme*, the
beginning of an endless series of reflections. The visual effect proclaims the nature of the image, while reinforcing its power. Dionysus is certainly present at the heart of the symposion: in liquid form
as the content of the krater, visually on the painted vase, and again
in liquid form as the imaginary content of the latter vessel. By using
a variety of graphic techniques—red figure, black silhouette, checkerboard—the painter gives concrete reality to the different levels of
figuration and to their hierarchical order.[23] The chromatic code blos-
soms in the play of visual echoes.

[23] The rest of the vase is decorated as follows: on the neck, with palmettes in red
figure; on the upper surface of the lip, with a race of riders and chariots in black

80. Red-figure pelike, Somzée painter, ca. 450.

Such graphic experiments are not very common, and it is not surprising to find that they are almost all connected with Dionysus or his entourage. Thus a *pelike* shows the god himself (identified by the kantharos he holds) reclining under a grape arbor in a rocky landscape sketched in a few strokes (fig. 80).[24] His company consists of a maenad standing to his right, who is carrying a tray loaded with grapes, and an aged satyr to the left, who is leaning on a staff. At the feet of the god is a youth holding a strainer and an oenochoe who is turning toward the krater from which he is about to draw a measure. The krater itself is decorated with the silhouettes of a maenad with a thyrsus and a dancing satyr: in their movement the two painted figures are animated versions of the static "real" figures flanking Dionysus. It is as if the painted scene is livelier than its putative subjects. Moreover, the representation of the god in a sit-

silhouette; under the handles, with a satyr and a Dionysus, also in black silhouette.
[24] Red-figure pelike: New York, 75.2.27 (GR593); Beazley, ARV 1159/2.

uation directly comparable to a human symposion—complete with couch, laden table, and of course the indispensable krater and cup bearer—creates, in the mirror game between the drinker and his image, a feeling of displacement. The scene depicted is a symposion, but it belongs to Dionysus. The primary image, on the amphora, embodies a metaphorical shift in relation to the context in which it is being used; we pass from the human banquet to the divine. The secondary image, in silhouette on the painted krater, embodies a second shift, as it propels into motion the old satyr who is standing, immobile, next to the krater. Hence the interplay of successive levels is not redundant; each stage returns to Dionysus and the enthusiasm inspired by wine.

Elsewhere the subject is the enthusiasm of the maenads, as expressed in their communal dance around a statue of Dionysus (fig. 81).[25] The whole surface of the cup is occupied by ten women, with their hair loosened, dancing to the music of a flute around a focal point consisting of an altar and a columnar statue. The statue is a pillar, barely visible at the base, to which a bearded mask of Dionysus has been attached.[26] The pillar is wrapped in a pleated robe; at shoulder height a number of branches support large round loaves. To the right of this portable idol is an altar, seen from the side, that is topped with a triangular pediment and a palmette. Under one of the handles, next to the signature of the potter Hieron, is a krater garlanded with ivy (see fig. 9). The space defined by this image is not that of a symposion but of a female festival linked to Dionysus and wine. On the back, three maenads carry wands tipped with ivy (*thyrsoi*); one is hoisting a fawn, another plays castanets (*krotala*), and yet another is carrying a skyphos, confirming the presence of wine at the ritual. The skyphos is decorated with a silhouetted border of ivy, two palmettes, and a satyr, who represents *en abîme* the masculine counterpart to Dionysus's female retinue.

The altar too has a visual pun, analogous to the other secondary image. The pediment shows a seated figure holding a staff and a branch—Dionysus. Thus the god appears twice, in his statue and in

[25] Red-figure cup: Berlin, 2290; Beazley, ARV 462/48.
[26] See J. L. Durand, F. Frontisi-Ducroux, "Idoles, figures, images: autour de Dionysos," *RA* (1982): 81–108.

81. Red-figure cup, Makron; signed Hieron potter, ca. 480.

the painted image atop the altar. One final detail is that the cloth around the pillar is richly embroidered, with chariots at the bottom and dolphins at the top. In the next chapter I will analyze the links among these familiar animals, Dionysus, and the sea.

The most striking feature here is the extraordinary density of imagistic play, which reaches out from a Dionysiac celebration to encompass satyrs, the god himself, and ocean life. The precision of such details also reminds us of the importance of the Greeks' visual environment; this one image assembles several different kinds of representational art—the statue, the painted altar, the embroidery, and the vase painting. These objects refer to one another and openly collaborate in an iconographic program that subtly reinforces the content of the scene painted on the cup.

It seems that the Greeks were very aware of the possibilities offered by this type of subliminal imagery, especially in the motifs (*episema*) emblazoned on warriors' shields. The scene of departure of the Seven against Thebes in Aeschylus's tragedy exemplifies this kind of semantic interplay, where each motif has meaning in relation to the individual hero carrying it, and the motifs taken together form a whole.[27] The tondo of a red figure cup provides remarkable evidence for this point of view (fig. 82).[28] It shows a young ephebe whirling to the music of a flute. He is carrying the peltast's light shield (see fig. 58) and, spear in hand, performs the armed dance called the *pyrrhikhe*, which was part of certain ritual occasions.[29] The ephebe's shield device seems to refer to this festal atmosphere; it shows a person dancing, as at a symposion, with a large krater at his feet. The shield's surface thus conveys the values of the banquet, of which the ephebes' dance sometimes was a part. In this tondo the mirror game between the drinker and his image does not take place directly on the vase, but at one remove, through the reference to the

---

[27] See F. Zeitlin, *Under the Sign of the Shield* (Rome, 1982), and P. Vidal-Naquet, "Les Boucliers des héros," in J.-P. Vernant and P. Vidal-Naquet, *Mythe et tragédie, deux* (Paris, 1986), 115–147.

[28] Red-figure cup: Lucerne market; Beazley, ARV 136/10.

[29] On the *pyrrhikhe*, see P. Scarpi, "La Pyrriche o le armi della persuasione," *D. Arch.* (1979): 78–97, and J.-C. Poursat, "Les Représentations de danse armée dans la céramique attique," BCH 92 (1968): 550–615.

82. Red-figure cup,
Poseidon painter, ca. 500.

ephebes' martial dance. Once again, the figural interplay proves to be unusually rich and complex, revealing both the importance of imagery at a symposion and the painters' awareness of this importance.

In its ingredients the symposion includes the image that circulates with the vases passed from hand to hand, along with wine, poetry, and music. It provides room for the expression of a culture that is as visual as it is verbal, based on an acquaintance with both picture and song. The imagery depends for its effect on the memory of the painters, who transmit and transform the iconographic motifs, and on the memory of the drinkers, who recognize the painted scenes and their own likenesses in the mirror of the vases.

Most evidence for the visual culture of the Greeks is lost: cloth has disappeared, paintings have disintegrated, most of the statues have been melted down or shattered. To understand Greek painting we must rely on the accounts of ancient travelers, which is like understanding Florentine painting on the basis of the comments in a guidebook for tourists. The ancient Greek world is wholly foreign to us, and writing the history of Greek painting means writing the history of a ghost made of words. Nonetheless, the vases do exist. They allow us to catch a glimpse of the importance of the image in Athenian culture, as they explore a range of representational effects in reflections direct, *en abîme*, and at one or more removes.

Naturally this impression results in part from the selection we have made from among the Athenian documents. Most of the images we have discussed appear on vases, cups, or kraters used for wine at symposia. In order to appreciate the self-reflexivity of the imagery, we must do our best to evaluate the whole repertoire. What role does the imagery of wine play in the world of painting? What are the major themes addressed by the painters of drinking vessels, and how often does each motif appear? The answers to such questions are not easy and would not fit within the scope of this essay, but the work of J. D. Beazley makes it possible to sketch some preliminary outlines.[30] By attributing the images, most of which are unsigned, to various "hands," this great British scholar provided a structure for the whole corpus of Athenian painted vases, distinguishing styles, putting the painters into groups, and showing their relations within the history of Athenian pottery. Thanks to Beazley's lists, we can determine the number of scenes devoted to one theme or another and gauge their relative importance.

We may begin with Douris.[31] There are about three hundred vases attributed to him; many are so fragmentary that we cannot specify the subject; among the rest, given that a complete cup has three scenes, there are a total of 387 scenes. Of these, 41 show a komos, and 42 a symposion, to which we may add 26 Dionysiac scenes; in all, almost a third of the surviving examples—a considerable proportion—have to do with wine. Many images depict conversations between men and women, or between men and youths; 106 pictures of this type treat the moment of meeting, of amorous banter and seduction. There are 50 scenes of athletes exercising, and

[30] It is difficult to gauge the relation between the Attic vases with attributions by Beazley and the whole corpus of known vases. The research being conducted at the Beazley archives in Oxford should soon allow for precise figures. A first attempt at thematic classification is to be found in T.B.L. Webster, *Potter and Patron in Classical Athens* (London, 1972), but although this study is based on Beazley's lists it does not deal with the painters.

[31] Beazley, ARV 427–448; D. Buitron, "Douris," Ph.D. diss. (New York, 1976).

62 of warriors arming themselves or in combat. Finally, 56 paintings show various mythological scenes.

Beazley attributes 339 vases to Makron;[32] leaving aside the fragments, there remain 425 complete scenes. Of the latter, there are 80 of the komos, 39 of the symposion, and 79 of Dionysiac activities, for a total of 198—almost half the surviving examples. There are also many scenes of encounters between men and women or men and youths: 137 in all. By contrast, there are very few athletes (22), even fewer warriors (7), and a relatively small number of mythological scenes (45). In comparing these two painters, we find that both devote an important percentage of their work to the komos and the symposion, and to scenes of conversation or meeting. The other themes are weighted differently, as Makron favors Dionysus and Douris athletes and warfare. The painters evidently made choices from the options available to them, but their work reflects the constraints imposed by the taste of their times; it reveals a preference for the symposion and the komos, and a portrayal of social relations, centered on wine, or taking place in the exercise hall, the agora, or the home of the music master or the courtesan.

It is worth extending this rapid survey to a painter who worked on large vases rather than cups. The Kleophrades painter is a fascinating case.[33] He is credited with 112 vases, from which 126 complete scenes are preserved. The largest single set (50) deals with mythological scenes, which is the opposite of what we saw with Douris and Makron. He has only one symposion, 6 instances of a komos, and 20 Dionysiac scenes; that is, one-fifth of his work is dedicated to wine, and especially to its god. There are 15 scenes of athletic activity, and 16 of warfare—this is the same ratio as that of Douris. There are 10 depictions of youths, and 4 of lyre players that have no parallel among the painted cups. The Kleophrades painter, then, clearly differs from the other two in the choices he makes, but the privileged place he accords Dionysus seems to be a response to

[32] Beazley, ARV 458–480; D. von Bothmer, "Notes on Makron," in *The Eye of Greece: Studies in Honor of Martin Robertson* (Oxford, 1982), 29–52.
[33] Beazley, ARV 181–192.

the apparent demand for imagery celebrating wine, the vine, and its god.

In addition to the significant number of paintings that treat wine and the symposion, it is noticeable how often the vases show athletes. One of the fundamental roles of the images is to display the beauty of the body, often emphasized by the use of the epithet *kalos*. Youthful beauty is seen as a gift of the gods, a sign of perfection in the divine order,[34] and when it is ideal, it is comparable to that of a statue. So it is when Plato describes the young Charmides:

> All of them, down to the very least child, turned and looked at him as if he had been a statue . . . Chairephon called me and said: "What do you think of him, Socrates? Has he not a beautiful face?" "That he has indeed," I said. "But you would think nothing of his face," he replied, "if you could see his naked form: he is absolutely perfect."[35]

The palaestra was where erotic relations were established between adults and young men. Theognis exclaims, "Happy the lover who frequents the gymnasium."[36] The athletes' exercise is a spectacle, and the palaestra was a kind of theater for the gratification of the sense of sight. The vase paintings reproduce and idealize such visual display and merge this dimension of Greek taste with the symposion.

In the same way, and in conclusion, the depictions of episodes from myth echo the poems recited at the symposion and share in the same culture. They are not simple illustrations, in the strict sense of the term, but reconsiderations in another medium, sometimes with important changes. Thus, at the symposion, painted imagery reflects both the guests' visual experience and their poetic memory.

[34] See J.-P. Vernant, *Myth and Thought among the Greeks* (Boston, 1983), and "Corps obscur, corps éclatant," in *Corps des Dieux. Le Temps de la Réflexion* 7 (1986): 19–45.
[35] Plato, *Charmides*, 153c and 154d, trans. Jowett. See H. I. Marrou, *Histoire de l'éducation dans l'Antiquité* 1 (Paris, 1981), 79–81.
[36] Theognis, 1335.

Chapter 6

Wine and the
Wine-Dark Sea

To denote the sea or describe its appearance, the Homeric poems often use the formula "the wine-dark sea," *oinops pontos*.[1] This metaphor linking the two liquids was widely known to, and elaborated by, the lyric poets.[2] Within Greek culture there are multiple analogies drawn among wine, the sea, navigation, and the symposion. In the poem sent to Thrasyboulos of Agrigentum, Pindar describes the carefree moment in a symposion when the guests steer toward a blissful utopia:

> Then the cares that exhaust men
> flee from their hearts; then, as on an ocean
> of wealth amidst gold in abundance,
> we row together toward an illusory shore;
> then the pauper is rich [. . .]
> our hearts swell, overcome by the curve of the vine.[3]

The assembled guests are like a ship's crew, departing together on the same crossing. A fragment from the poet Dionysos Chalchos describes the guests as rowers for Dionysus:

---

[1] For example, *Od.*, 5.13e, 221; 7.250, etc.

[2] See W. Slater, "Symposion at Sea," HSCP 80 (1976): 161–170, and "Peace, the Symposion and the Poet," ICS 6 (1981): 205–214; J. Péron, *Les Images maritimes de Pindare* (Paris, 1974); and especially the superb article by M. Davies, "Sailing, Rowing and Sporting in One's Cup on the Wine-Dark Sea," in *Athens Comes of Age: from Solon to Salamis* (Princeton, 1978), 72–90.

[3] Pindar *ap.* Athenaeus, 11.480c (= fr. 124 Snell).

some, carrying wine in Dionysus's crew,
seamen of the symposion, rowers of the cup [. . .].

Since this passage is only partially quoted by Athenaeus,[4] it is not
possible to grasp the full meaning of the metaphor, but the interplay
between the wine and the sea, and between a ship and the banquet
hall, is quite clear. Similarly, when Heracles praises a life of feasting
in Euripides' *Alcestis* and mentions the rhythmic pulse of the cup
that one raises to one's lips, he uses the word *pitulos*, which refers to
the rower's pull on his oar.[5] Finally, a broken cup symbolizes a recent shipwreck, as in the following passage from Choerilos:

> I have in my hand a piece of a cup, totally smashed,
> the remains of a shipwreck of guests, like the one
> caused by Dionysus's powerful gale, which propels us
> toward the shores of Unreason.[6]

This powerful gale, this wind of drunkenness, often capsizes the
drinker:

> I'm starting to nod off;
> that cup I drank in honor of Zeus the Savior
> has completely wrecked me, the sailor, and sent me
> to the bottom, as you can see.[7]

It is easy for all these drinkers to put wind in their sails. Athenaeus, who is the source for most of these quotations, has at the
beginning of his work a racy story that depends on the same analogies and compares sailors and drinkers:

> Timaeus of Tauromenium says that in Agrigentum there is a house
> which is called the "trireme" from the following circumstance. A
> party of young fellows were drinking in it, and became so wild
> when overheated by the liquor that they imagined they were sailing
> in a trireme, and that they were in a bad storm on the ocean. Fi-
> nally, they completely lost their senses, and tossed all the furniture

---

[4] Dionysos Chalchos *ap.* Athenaeus, 10.443c (= fr. 5 West).
[5] Euripides, *Alcestis*, 789.
[6] Choerilos *ap.* Athenaeus, 11.464b (= fr. 9 Kinkel).
[7] Xenarchos *ap.* Athenaeus, 15.693b (= fr. 3 Kock).

and bedding out of the house as though upon the waters, convinced that the pilot directed them to lighten the ship because of the raging storm. Well, a great crowd gathered and began to carry off the jetsam, but even then the youngsters did not cease from their mad actions. The next day the military authorities appeared at the house and made complaint against the young men when they were still half-seas over. To the questions of the magistrates they answered that they had been much put to it by a storm and had been compelled to throw into the seas the superfluous cargo. When the authorities expressed surprise at their insanity, one of the young men, though he appeared to be the eldest of the company, said to them, "Ye Tritons, I was so frightened that I threw myself into the lowest possible place in the hold and lay there." The magistrates, therefore, pardoned their delirium, but sentenced them never to drink too much, and let them go. They gratefully promised. . . . "If," said he, "we ever make port after this awful tempest, we shall rear altars in our country to you, as Saviors in visible presence, side by side with the sea gods, because you appeared to us so opportunely." This is why the house was called the "trireme."[8]

For these drunkards, what had been a mere metaphor is transformed into reality. Deceived by the wine they consumed, they no longer distinguish between fact and fantasy and reverse the relation between the two levels. The Dionysiac illusion, at full force, leads them to their ruin. This story is a comic version of what happens to queen Agave in Euripides' *Bacchae*. In the grip of Dionysiac frenzy, she slays her son Pentheus, thinking that she is slaughtering a lion. Dionysus controls this kind of blindness, whose forms can vary. In Euripides' tragedy, Dionysus punishes Pentheus for his refusal to believe in and accept the god; in the comic adventure of the Agrigentine youths, Dionysus transforms the banquet hall into a ship lost at sea. Though no real metamorphosis has taken place, Dionysus capitalizes on the power of metaphors; he strikes the young men with madness—*mania*—so that thereafter they are unable to perceive reality and remain locked into their delusion. The game lasts throughout the story, without a return to normalcy, until the final valedictory, when the magistrates are mistaken for savior gods who

---

[8] Timaeos *ap*. Athenaeus, 2.37b–e (= FGrHist 566), trans. Gulick.

have appeared on earth (*epiphaneis*). Dionysus himself is the god of stunning epiphanies.[9] It must have been quite a giddy trireme in Agrigentum.

Beyond the poetic metaphors that overzealous drinkers take literally, Greek, like English, can play on the multiple meanings of the word "vessel." A number of vases have ships' names, and the comic poets exploit this ambiguity in punning uses of the words *akatos*, *kymbion*, *olkas*, *trieres*, all of which can mean both a kind of pottery and a kind of ship.[10] The word "kantharos" itself is strongly polyvalent; it means the two-handled vase of Dionysus (see figs. 7, 76); it is also the name for a kind of beetle, as well as an area in the port of Piraeus—maritime space again—and, finally, one of the Giants who, on the frieze of the Siphnian treasury at Delphi, is carrying a helmet decorated with a vase in the shape of a kantharos—thus the cycle of verbal analogies finds visual closure.[11]

We could extend this game with the word "skyphos," a deep cup, which has two verbal associations: *skyphos/skythes*, Scythian—for the Scythians were the champions at drinking unmixed wine[12]—and *skyphos/skaphos*, ship's hull, which occurs in Euripides' *Cyclops* when the title character reels out of his cave after having drunk the wine Odysseus gave him:

> Am I crammed with wine!
> . . . The hold of my little dory
> is stuffed right up to the gunwales![13]

An English speaker can "drain a glass," while the Greek could "bail out a cup."[14] A similar metaphor recurs on a small vase (fig.

[9] On this aspect of Dionysus, see M. Detienne, *Dionysos at Large*.

[10] For these terms, see Athenaeus, 11: *naus*, 474b; *akatos*, 482f; *kymbion*, 481f; *olkas*, 481c; *trieres*, 500f. See also, in the accounts of Delphi, the less precise mention of *krateres trieretikoi* (ID, no. 104, I.131).

[11] Aristophanes, *Peace*, 145, and scholia *ad loc*. For the Delphic frieze, see E. Mastrokostas, "Zu den Namenbeischriften des Siphnier-Frieses," MDAI(A) 71 (1976): 74–82.

[12] For the Scythians, see chap. 1, n. 17; Anacreon *ap*. Athenaeus, 10.427a–b (= fr. 11/356 Page) and Achaios *ap*. Athenaeus, 10.427c. The verbal associations are found at Athenaeus, 11.499e–f.

[13] Euripides, *Cyclops*, 505–506, trans. Arrowsmith.

[14] Pherecrates *ap*. Athenaeus, 6.269c (= fr. 108,31 Kock).

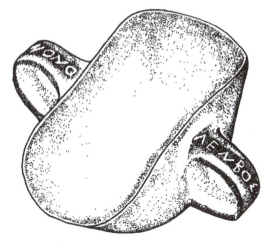

83. Black glazed cup, fifth century.

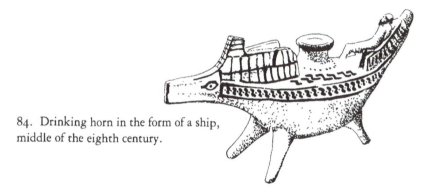

84. Drinking horn in the form of a ship,
middle of the eighth century.

83), undecorated but completely glazed, whose handles have the
inscription *lembos onoma*, "my name is skiff."[15] The vase's smooth
shape vaguely recalls that of a dinghy. As we have seen, the game of
kottabos could make use of little saucers floating in a liquid like
small boats, that could be sunk with a jet of wine.[16]

On occasion the potter quite explicitly modeled his vase after
a ship. For example, a sculpted geometric vase consists of a hull
resting on three legs (fig. 84).[17] The prow is decorated with an

[15] Frankfurt; R. Hackl, *Münchener Archäologische Studien* (Studies in Honor of
A. Furtwängler, Munich, 1910), 104.

[16] See chap. 4, pp. 80–86, and Athenaeus, 15.667e.

[17] Boston, 99.515; A Fairbanks, *Catalogue* (1928), no. 227, p. 83. Cf. also Paris,
Louvre CA577; CVA 17 (26), pl. 22 (1145), 3–4, and pp. 27–28.

85. Red-figure cup,
manner of Douris, ca. 490.

apotropaic eye, as are some other cups. On the deck the place of the
mast is taken by a raised opening through which the vessel can be
filled; it can be emptied through a spout in the stern. The order of
the elements is reversed; instead of a ship floating on the ocean, we
have wine pouring out of a hull.

Heracles the master drinker borrows a ship of this kind during one of his labors (the tenth in the list compiled by Apollodoros).[18] He had to go beyond the ocean to the island of Erythia and
steal the cattle of Geryon, the triple-bodied giant. Scorched by the
sun, the impatient hero tried to extinguish it by shooting it with
his arrows; admiring his audacity, the Sun gave him a golden vase
in which he might ride across the ocean. A red figure vase shows
him, with his bow in hand and his club resting on his shoulder, as
he sails in a large *dinos* above a fish-filled sea (fig. 85; see also fig.
10).[19] Once again this image produces visual effects at a number of
different levels: in the tondo of a cup is an image of a mixing bowl;
but instead of wine, the vase contains Heracles and floats on the
"wine-dark sea." During this miraculous crossing, container and
contents have reversed the positions they would usually occupy.

From time to time the painters literalize the metaphor of the
"wine-dark sea" by converting the interior of vases for wine into

[18] Ps.-Apollodoros, *Bibl.*, 2.10.4.
[19] Red-figure cup: Vatican; Beazley, ARV 449/2.

86. Black-figure dinos, ca. 510.

nautical spaces. The necks of certain kraters—not outside, facing the drinkers, but inside, facing the liquid—are decorated with friezes of long boats circling the mixed wine (fig. 86).[20] When the vase is full, the surface of the liquid is flush with the triremes, which seem to float on the wine in which they are reflected. Thus the liquid becomes a mirror that doubles the painted image and reinforces the visual illusion. Wine becomes sea, and metaphor becomes reality; before the eyes of the guests, the joint action of the wine and the painting transforms a Homeric formula into a lifelike vision.

The same effect can be found on a cup intended for the use of a single drinker (fig. 87).[21] Its interior is decorated with a continuous row of four ships, while the tondo shows a young reveler carrying an amphora. Dolphins leap between the ships, giving the image a heightened sense of movement. We can imagine the effect pro-

[20] Red-figure dinos: Boston, 90.154; CVA 2 (19), pl. 66 (900), and text on pp. 9–10.
[21] Red-figure cup: London, BM E2; Beazley, ARV 225/1. See K. Schauenburg, "Zu attisch-schwarzfiguren Schalen mit Innenfriesen," *AntK Beiheft* 7 (1970): 33–40, and p. 34, n. 21, for the ship kraters.

87. Red-figure cup, painter of London E2, ca. 490.

duced by the ships sailing on the wine within the cup. A mixture of graphic techniques—black figure for the ships, red figure for the youth—creates a neat division between the two motifs. The cup's black surface, highlighted by the dark color of the wine, forms a continuum with the ships. The youth is isolated in his tondo, on a higher plane. The two images correspond to one another—connecting navigation with the transport of wine in the amphora—but they cannot be blended. Such a juxtaposition of elements contains enough poetic resonance for the metaphorical process to occur. The painter associates wine with ships and with the amphora carrier; once the image has been charged with wine, it will go into action under the drinker's gaze.

Other vases allow for a different kind of play with the reflection of images in the wine. So it is with the psykter, the cooling vase designed to be immersed in a krater (see fig. 77). Its bowl, almost spherical in shape, is mounted on a fairly tall cylinder that functions both as a base and a kind of keel (see fig. 78). The psykters are rare. They were in style for only a short period, and they seem to connote luxury, a sophisticated approach to the act of drinking, and a noticeable refinement in table manners. Their decoration depicts some athletes, a few mythological scenes, most often Dionysus at a symposion or in a procession.

A psykter attributed to the painter Oltos demonstrates true mastery in the art of arranging images (fig. 88).[22] It shows six men riding dolphins. Each rider is bearded, helmeted, and armed with a shield, breastplate, and greaves; each is preceded by the same inscription in front of his mouth, *epidelphinos*, "mounted on a dolphin." These warriors in hoplite armor define themselves by calling themselves knights in a special corps. When the cooling vase is placed in a krater, the warriors are reflected in the liquid, and the dolphins look as if they were swimming through the wine-dark sea. The circle of drinking guests, citizen-soldiers of Athens, is met by its own image: not the knights of the Athenian aristocracy but a retinue of six warriors riding in single file through the drinkable depths.[23] The emblems on their shields form two distinct sets: one series is of vases, a cup (*kylix*), a krater, and a kantharos; the other is a series of circular designs, three legs, three winged animals (lion, horse, gryphon), and a wheel with four spokes whose rim is formed of dolphins.[24] The image of the dolphin appears *en abîme*, as a turning wheel, as if to heighten the circular effect of the drawings that revolve on the discs of the shields.

The set of vases for wine brings forth all the aspects of a symposion: the krater for mixing, the kylix for drinking, and the kantharos for the presence of Dionysus. The vase shapes are as meaning-

[22] Red-figure psykter: New York, Schimmel collection, on loan to the Metropolitan Museum of Art, L.1979.17.1; Beazley, ARV 1622/7 twice, *Para* 326; A. Greifenhagen, "Delphinreiter auf einem Psykter des Oltos," *Pantheon* 23 (1965): 1–7. See, in general, chap. 5, esp. n. 20.

[23] The Greek verb *thoresso*, "to arm with a breastplate," can also be used in the middle-passive to mean a drunkard; see Theognis, 470 and 413.

[24] For these emblems, see G. H. Chase, *The Shield Devices of the Greeks* (Cambridge, Mass., 1902). For the circular patterns, see Beazley, "An Amphora by the Berlin Painter," *AntK* 4 (1961): 58–67.

88. Red-figure psykter, Oltos, ca. 510.

ful as the circular motifs, because they represent the egalitarian circulation of wine under the aegis of Dionysus. Far from being purely decorative, this double series juxtaposes the space of the symposion with that of warfare, much like the youth dancing the war dance (*pyrrhikhe*) or some satyrs (see fig. 82). The community of men—that is, of citizens (see fig. 58)—reasserts itself again and again by means of two collective actions, the symposion and warfare, which have certain similarities, are to some degree interdependent, and refer to one another through the play of reflections in the wine. Finally, the image privileges various types of circularity: the motifs on the shields, the shields themselves, and the warriors making their rounds on their dolphins. The last of these recapitulates in the world of war one of the most important features of the symposion: the equality among guests that parallels the equality among hoplites in the line of battle.

This band of knights on dolphins is not unique. On occasion the warriors' motion, like the hoplites' advance on a battlefield, gets its cadence from the music of a flute (fig. 89).[25] Here the flute player is not female, as at a procession of drinkers, but a male wearing a long tunic, like those who play during athletic competitions or musical events. Now the group resembles a chorus, much like the birds or knights we find in Old Comedy.[26] It is not necessary, however, to reduce the whole set of warriors on dolphins to this single level,

[25] Black-figure lekythos; Palermo, Banco di Sicilia; *Odeon*, pl. 51 and pl. XI. Cf. the black-figure lekythos: Athens; Beazley, ABV 518/2.
[26] See G. M. Sifakis, *Parabasis and Animal Choruses* (London, 1971), and the recent article by J. R. Green, "A Representation of the *Birds* of Aristophanes," in *Greek Vases in the J. Paul Getty Museum* 2 (1985): 95–118.

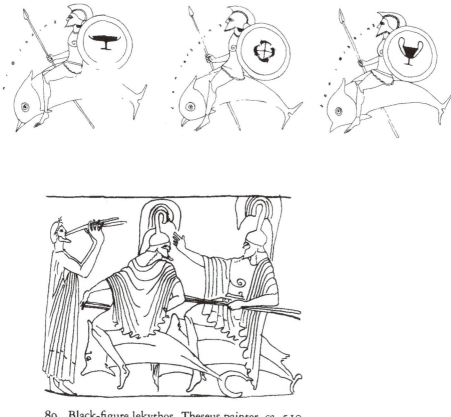

89. Black-figure lekythos, Theseus painter, ca. 510.

or to assume that they all refer to dramatic choruses. When the great psykter, with its band of six riders, is set into the wine in front of the drinkers, it draws attention not to its theatricality but to the utopian space of the oceanic wine.

A similar space appears on a lekythos that shows two nude ephebes riding on dolphins alongside a rocky island occupied by a crouching satyr (fig. 90).[27] Dionysus's colleague is holding out a pitcher to refill the cup of the rider on the left. The distribution of wine takes place in a kind of dressage whose focus is the central crag; in this imaginary space, the rock occupies the place of the krater in the midst of the guests.

As a conveyance to this utopian realm, the dolphin is not

[27] Black-figure lekythos: Baltimore; CVA 1 (4), pl. 37 (170) 3.

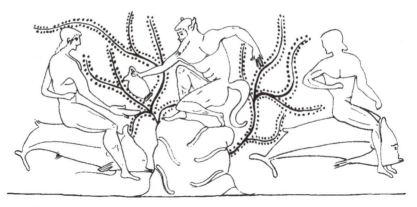

90. Black-figure lekythos, ca. 510.

chosen by accident. Several accounts present it as a creature friendly to man; it serves as a guide for his ships and often saves him from drowning and carries him to shore. When the poet Arion was captured by pirates, he asked that before he was killed he be allowed to sing one last time; the dolphins, which appreciated music more than the pirates did, recovered the poet from the sea and brought him safely to Cape Taenarum.[28] In discussing the intelligence of these animals, Plutarch observes:

> It is the only creature who loves man for his own sake. Of the land animals, some avoid man altogether, others, the tamest kind, pay court for utilitarian reasons only to those who feed them. . . . To the dolphin alone, beyond all others, nature has granted what the best philosophers seek: friendship for no advantage. Though it has no need at all of any man, yet it is a genial friend to all and has helped many. The story of Arion is familiar to everyone and widely known.[29]

Among those who are found riding on dolphins is Eros, a winged youth who controls his mount by means of reins or by playing a flute, as if in response to its fondness for music (figs. 91, 92).[30]

[28] Herodotus, 1.23–24.
[29] Plutarch, *De sollertia animalium*, 36.984c, trans. Helmbold. See E. Stebbins, *The Dolphin in Literature and Art of Greece and Rome* (Menasha, 1929).
[30] Red-figure cup: Palermo, 1518; unattributed; A. Greifenhagen, *Griechische Eroten* (Berlin, 1957), fig. 26.

91. Red-figure cup, ca. 500.

92. Red-figure lekythos,
Bowdoin painter, ca. 490.

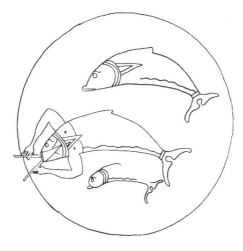

93. Black-figure cup, ca. 570.

Such an image joins two of the basic elements of a symposion: the flute music that accompanies the singing of the guests, and Eros, whose praises often provide the topic for conversation.[31] Dolphins so love the sound of the flute, the *aulos*, that even their bodies say so: in Greek, the term for the dolphin's breathing hole is "aulos."

There is more: the tondo of a cup shows three dolphins of different sizes (fig. 93).[32] The middle one has been given arms and

[31] F. Lasserre, "Erotikoi logoi," *MH* (1944): 169–176.

[32] Black-figure cup: Rome, Villa Giulia 64 608; E. Simon, *Die griechischen Vasen* (Munich, 1976), 78–79, pl. 61. For other metamorphoses, see E. Rohde, *AA* (1955), cols. 102–111.

hands, which are holding the twin tubes of a flute. In addition, its face is partially covered by a leather strip that masks its cheeks and mouth, a *phorbeia*, used by human flutists to control the flow of air into the instrument. In this metamorphosis, the dolphin is no longer guided by the flute but itself has become a flute player. The boundary between human and animal becomes more and more tenuous; this wine-dark sea, placed in the drinker's grasp, harbors an astonishing beast; once again the image takes literally the metaphor of the music-loving dolphin and transforms it into reality through graphic play. The dolphin becomes a musician, like the poem in which Pindar compares himself to a dolphin:

> I feel the urge to sing,
> and I answer the call like the dolphin
> when, in the vast empty ocean,
> he is moved by the flute's sweet song.[33]

To conclude this survey we may consider a famous cup signed by Exekias, which is unique in several ways (fig. 94).[34] The whole interior, not just a tondo, portrays a ship surrounded by seven leaping dolphins. The ship, however, is not altogether normal. A tremendous vine springs from the bridge; twined around the mast that serves as its support, it spreads wide and carries seven bunches of grapes, equal in number to the dolphins capering around the vessel, which is itself decorated with an eye and small dolphins in white. The ship has neither crew nor pilot, but a single captain, Dionysus, who is crowned with ivy and holds a drinking horn. He reclines at full length on the deck, as at a banquet table.

The mast and the vine, the ship and the symposiast's couch are completely intermingled. This picture has often been connected with the Homeric hymn to Dionysus, which tells how the god, traveling in disguise, is captured by pirates who intend to hold him for ransom. The pilot alone suspects that the prisoner might be a deity and tries to intervene, but to no avail. Then the fetters holding the god drop off, wine flows on the deck, a grapevine covers the ship

[33] Pindar, fr. 140b 15 Snell.
[34] Black-figure cup: Munich, 2044; Beazley, ABV 146/21. See M. Daraki, "Oinops pontos; la mer dionysiaque," RHR (1982): 3–22.

94. Black-figure cup, Exekias, ca. 540.

and clings to the mast; the sailors jump into the sea and are transformed into dolphins.[35] On the Exekias cup we find the dolphins and the spreading vine, but the pilot is missing, and the correspondence with the Homeric hymn is not one-for-one. Nonetheless, it is clear that we are witnessing a triumphant epiphany of Dionysus. Some details of technique reinforce this impression: the painting is not confined, as it would usually be, to a tondo; rather, all the available space is occupied by the god. The surface of the sea is not marked, and the dolphins go as high as the branches of the vine; the

[35] *Homeric Hymn to Dionysus*, 1.34–42, 52–53.

circular space of the cup is, in a way, limitless. Finally, the glaze on this vase is not black but a kind of coral-red that is created by a particular technique of firing; this shade emphasizes the visual effect of the color of the wine.[36]

Thus Dionysus triumphs: a symposiast on the wine-dark sea, lord of plant life and ocean life, and likewise master of metamorphoses and of metaphors that become visions.

[36] On this technique, see B. Cohen, "Observations on Coral-Red," *Marsyas* 15 (1970–71): 1–12.

Chapter 7

Song and Image

At the symposion, drinking and singing go hand in hand; poetry and wine are so closely linked that each can become a metaphor for the other. Pindar begins one of his odes:

> As in the splendor of a revel of men,
> we mix a second bowl of the strains of the Muses . . .
>   May the third time be
> such that we make at Aigina our last libation
> to Zeus Savior, Olympian, in the honeyed singing.[1]

In another place he addresses the person who will perform his choral poem:

> You are a true messenger . . .
> sweet mixing bowl of vociferous song.[2]

Choral performance, which brings together poetry, song and dance, is similar to the mixing that takes place in the krater. Wine is one of the metaphors Pindar uses most frequently in speaking of his odes. The poetic text circulates from the poet to the guests for whom it is intended; a poem can be offered like a drink, and verses are passed around like goblets. Dionysos Chalchos uses the same image:

---

[1] Pindar, *Isthmian*, 6.1–2, trans. Lattimore.
[2] Pindar, *Olympian*, 6.90–91, trans. Lattimore; see also *Nemean*, 3.78–79.

> Theodorus, receive this poem pledged as a toast from me;
> I send it on its right course to thee first of our company,
> mixing in the cup of the Graces the graces of friendship.

And again:

> Pour out the praise-songs like wine, for yourself and for us,
> passing them from left to right.[3]

The complementarity of wine and song was not unknown to the vase painters, who also attend to the poetry of the symposion. There are many images of singing, usually accompanied by the lyre or the flute (see figs. 9, 68, 73). In the musical culture of the Greeks, the symposion and the komos are the two most important occasions for the development of a whole range of poetic forms. The Homeric poems describe specialized singers, who are inspired by the Muses; after a feast, they accompany themselves on a lyre as they sing the grand epic sagas of heroes and their adventures. By the sixth century, however, the musical forms of the symposion have changed. The performers are no longer *aedoi* (composers) or *rhapsodoi* (chanters), but choruses or even the guests themselves, whose education should enable them to sing at such events. New genres of poetic expression arose: lyric poetry (great choral odes), elegiac poetry (with moral, political, or didactic themes), and popular song. Such poetry is basically written for the banquet: "The history of lyric is the history of the symposion."[4]

In depicting the symposion, therefore, the painters were naturally drawn to showing song, poetry, and music. The poet Simonides very early put the two levels, visual and acoustic, side by side, when he asked himself about the relationships between words and things, between pictures and poems. He is credited with two oft-

---

[3] Dionysos Chalchos *ap.* Athenaeus, 15.669e (= fr. 1.1 West), trans. Gulick.

[4] L. Rossi observes, "La storia della lirica è la storia del simposio" ("Il simposio greco," 49). On the connections between the symposion and lyric poetry, in addition to the studies by Rossi see B. Gentili, *Poesia e publico nella Grecia antica* (Rome-Bari, 1984); M. Vetta, ed., *Poesia e simposio nella Grecia antica; guida storica e critica* (Rome-Bari, 1983); G. Giangrande, "Sympotic Literature and Epigram," in *L'Epigramme grecque*, Entretiens sur l'Antiquité classique, Fondation Hardt XIV, (Geneva, 1968), 93–117.

95. Red-figure kalathos, Brygos painter, ca. 470.

cited observations: "The word (*logos*) is the image (*eikon*) of things"; "Painting is silent poetry, and poetry is talkative painting."[5]

In Simonides the contrast between the two forms of expression corresponds to an obvious taste for a striving after visual effect and colorful description, as if the two arts had the same aesthetic goal.[6] What do we find of poetry in the paintings?

To portray music and poetry in images, the painters did not merely show singers but sometimes—rarely, to be sure—tried to be more specific about the song itself. A singular vase shows the two great poets of Lesbos, Sappho and Alcaeus, standing next to each other (fig. 95).[7] Alcaeus is singing, and Sappho is turning back to

[5] Simonides *ap.* Michael Psellos, p. 821 Migne, and Plutarch, *Glor. Ath.* 3, *Mor.* 347a. See M. Bowra, *Greek Lyric Poetry* (Oxford, 1961), 363, and J. Svenbro, *La parola e il marmo* (Turin, 1984), chap. 5.
[6] It seems that Sophocles himself was aware of this question but that he strove instead to contrast the two modes of expression, verbal and visual. See Athenaeus, 13.603e–604c.
[7] Red-figure kalathos: Munich, 2416; Beazley, ARV 385/228.

listen to him. Each of them is holding a long lyre (*barbiton*) in the left hand and a plectrum in the right. These two figures are not portraits but, like many others, images of musicians. The identification of the individuals that takes this scene out of the ordinary is created by the inscriptions that appear next to Alcaeus's head and alongside Sappho's neck. A vertical inscription reads *damakalos*, "Damas is beautiful." Finally, a string of five O's in front of Alcaeus's mouth indicates that he is singing.

The use of writing here shows a great deal of variety, and even though the four inscriptions are equally melded into the image, they have three different ranks. The vertical inscription is outside the image and, we might say, parasitical on it; the two proper names next to the heads are captions, or rather labels that identify the two poets and are like their attributes. Finally, the string of vowels before the singer's mouth is the graphic equivalent of his song, the visual symbol of his melody. This vocal notation makes the inscription an object that resounds, parallel to the instrument that accompanies it. The painter has not quoted the poet's words but has only suggested a sound without linguistic content.

In the richness of its graphics this image offers two solutions to the problem of integrating poetry into painting: give the poet's name, and transcribe his song. The former solution is very rare in vase painting, where portraiture is nonexistent. In addition to this Sappho and Alcaeus, we have a few contemporary images that identify a figure as the poet Anacreon, but again we may conclude that this is more a matter of referring to a certain type of song and a particular kind of life than of accurately depicting the poet himself.[8] Homer, who pervades Athenian life, does not appear on a single vase. We do find the legendary poet Orpheus, either charming the barbarian Thracians or being brutally slaughtered by their companions,[9] but then we are very far from the symposion, that harbor of tranquility.

[8] On this point, see F. Frontisi-Ducroux and F. Lissarrague, "From Ambiguity to Ambivalence."
[9] For this theme, see M. Schmitt, "Der Tod des Orpheus . . . ," *AntK*, *Neuntes Beiheft* (Berne, 1973): 95–105.

96. Red-figure amphora, Smikros, ca. 510.

97. Black-figure epinetron, Sappho painter, ca. 500.

The other solution, the acoustic, is more common. Some inscriptions are associated with musical instruments and seem to function onomatopoetically. Thus a flute-playing satyr, appropriately named Terpaulos—"the one who charms with his flute"[10]—is accompanied by a vertical text of nonsense syllables: *netenareneteneto* (fig. 96). These sounds resemble a series of notes and seem to emerge from the flute itself.

Another, fragmentary image shows some Amazons arming themselves in preparation for war. One of them is playing a trumpet[11] and is surrounded by the repeated syllables *totote, tote*, which are meaningless but could well be real musical notation (fig. 97).[12]

[10] Red-figure amphora: Berlin, inv. 1966.19; Beazley, *Para* 323/3 twice (see chap. 2, n. 35).
[11] Black-figure epinetron: Eleusis, 907; Haspels, ABL 228/54.
[12] See A. Belis, "Un nouveau document musical," BCH 108 (1984): 99–109.

98. Black-figure skyphos, Pistias class, ca. 515.

Such incomprehensible texts are fairly common in the images from the end of the sixth and the beginning of the fifth century. Sometimes they are purely decorative and are used to fill empty space in the picture or to substitute for meaningful writing. In certain instances, the meaning of the inscription resides in its graphic, not linguistic, aspect.[13]

In a painting of a seated man playing a lyre, the inscription does not even reach the level of onomatopoea—he is singing, with his mouth open, and in front of him is a trail of unintelligible signs, partially formed letters, or mere dots and dashes (fig. 98).[14] The inscription is reduced to a trajectory; like water spewing from the mouth of a gargoyle, the letters run together in a stream down to the singer's feet.

More often the inscription is readable, and the singer's words make sense. In the tondo of a cup (fig. 99),[15] a young guest reclines,

[13] F. Lissarrague, "Graphein: Ecrire et dessiner sont identiques en leur fond," in C. Bérard, ed., *Images en jeu* (Lausanne, 1988).

[14] Black-figure skyphos: Elvehjem Museum of Art, Madison, 1979.122; W. G. Moon, *Greek Vase Paintings in Mid-Western Collections* (Chicago, 1979), no. 70, p. 123.

[15] Red-figure cup: Florence, 3949; Beazley, ARV 376/90.

99. Red-figure cup,
Brygos painter, ca. 480.

with his outstretched right hand holding a bough of myrtle, and he sings *pile kai*, "love and. . . ."[16] The track of the song leads from his mouth toward his hand, and only the first two words are recorded. The result is a complex sense of movement: the direction of the writing makes the words come from the singer's mouth, and the fact that the inscription is interrupted shows that the words are in the process of being spoken. The youth's gesture corresponds to the custom of group singing at a symposion. We know that it was a sort of relay, "as a myrtle branch is passed from left to right,"[17] and that each guest sang in turn on a given topic or continued a song begun by his neighbor. This form of singing is called *scolion*, a word that conveys the sinuous nature of the activity, making its way from one guest to the other.[18]

Among the scraps of poetry that the images preserve, we also find references to the gods. A fragmentary cup shows a bearded guest chanting *opollon*, "O Apollo" (fig. 100).[19] A shield decorated with a bird and a pair of greaves are hooked together in front of him; we rarely find depictions of armor in this period, but a passage from

[16] In this inscription the letter *pi* replaces *phi*; see P. Kretschmer, *Die griechischen Vaseninschriften* (Gütersloh, 1894), par. 48, pp. 81, 230.
[17] Pollux, 6.108.
[18] Plutarch, *Table Talk*, 1.1.5. See Aristophanes, *Wasps*, 1219–1249, and the songs quoted by Athenaeus, 15.694c–696a.
[19] Red-figure cup: Paris, Cabinet des médailles 546; Beazley, ARV 372/26.

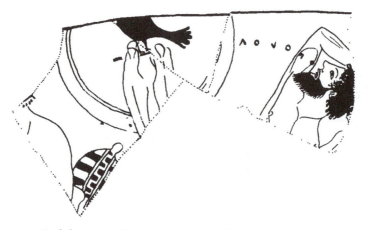

100. Red-figure cup, Brygos painter, ca. 480.

Alcaeus describes weapons as part of an exhortation to martial valor.[20] The invocation of Apollo matches what we find, for example, at the beginning of Plato's *Symposium*:

> Socrates took his place on the couch; and when the meal was ended, and the libations offered, and after a hymn had been sung to the god [Apollo], and there had been the usual ceremonies, they were about to commence drinking.[21]

In the same way Theognis calls upon Olympian Zeus and Apollo, god of the banquet:

> May Zeus who lives in the ether always extend his hand
> over this city, to preserve it,
> and the other beneficent gods with him. May Apollo
> guide our words and our thoughts.
> May the *phorminx* and the flute let us hear a holy melody;
> and finally may we, after we have poured libations to the gods,
> drink, talking happily with one another,
> with no more fear of the warlike attack of the Medes.[22]

Brief as it may be on the fragment of the cup, the salute to Apollo recalls the ritual quality of the symposion.

[20] Alcaeus *ap.* Athenaeus, 14.627a–b (= fr. Z34 Lobel-Page).
[21] Plato, *Symposium*, 176a, trans. Jowett.
[22] Theognis, 757–764.

101. Red-figure cup, Douris, ca. 480.

Other remarks have an earthier character. A bearded drinker, for example, holds his cup and sings *oudunamou*, "I can't . . .";[23] his sentence remains unfinished, and we will never know exactly what he cannot do (fig. 101). This image has been compared to some lines of Theognis where the poet complains that he is no longer able to sing because he has celebrated too much, but we can also imagine several other kinds of debility for this drinker whose utterance is broken off. His posture is worth noting: his head is thrown back, and his arm is raised so as to free his chest and expose his throat. To have the neck bent back is typical of a certain kind of Dionysiac ecstasy, as the chorus says in Euripides' *Bacchae*:

> Will the time come
> when barefoot I tread the nightlong dances, in ecstasy
> flinging back my head in the clean dewy air?[24]

Evoking a festival in honor of Dionysus, Pindar alludes to:

> The delirious cries, the shouts
> that accompany the sudden shake of the head thrown back.[25]

[23] Red-figure cup: Munich, 2646; Beazley, ARV 437/128. For the inscription, cf. Theognis, 939–940.
[24] Euripides, *Bacchae*, 862–864, trans. Dodds. See the commentaries by Dodds and J. Roux *ad loc*.
[25] Pindar *ap*. Plutarch, *Table Talk*, 7.6.706e (= fr. D2.13 Snell).

102. Red-figure cup, ca. 490.

In the painting, the position of the head allows the drinker to give full voice to the song he sings to the music of a flute.[26]

We see this same pose held by another symposiast (fig. 102), whose beard points upward as he exclaims *o paidon kalliste*, "O most beautiful boy."[27] Once again the text emerges from the figure's mouth and follows the curve of the tondo, as if to fill the whole space with sound. The singer's left hand holds castanets, while the right strokes a hare, which is one of the gifts an adult can offer a youth whose beauty he admires.[28] Touching the animal is a substitute for touching the beloved, and the gesture is amplified by the song that extols the young man's matchless beauty, as in some verses of Theognis:

> Most beautiful and most entrancing of youths,
> listen, as you stand there, to some words from my mouth.[29]

The painters do not reserve a special place for the text of the song, nor do they try to separate it out by means of some device like the balloons in our comic strips that detach the words from the draw-

[26] For this gesture, see the examples collected by E. Vermeule, "Fragments of a Symposion by Euphronios," *AntK* 8 (1965): 34–39.
[27] Red-figure cup: Athens, MN1357; unattributed; MDAI(A) 9 (1884), pl. 1.
[28] See A. Schnapp, "Eros the Hunter," in C. Bérard et al., *A City of Images*, 71–88.
[29] Theognis, 1365–1366.

103. Red-figure amphora, Euphronios, ca. 520.

ings. On the contrary, the trajectory of the inscription traces a line in the image and gives it some of its dynamism.

The same is true of a painting on an amphora that shows a lyre player reclining as he sings *mamekapoteo*,[30] which could mean "I suffer from longing," as in a famous poem by Sappho (fig. 103).[31] Here the letters form a kind of halo around the head of the singer, who looks as if he is caught in his own song. This positioning is clearly marked off from the tilt of another inscription to the left, *leagros kalos*, "Leagros is beautiful." The latter exists outside the image and repeats the praise of a young man who is often named on the vases of this time (see figs. 21, 25).[32] The salute to a handsome youth and the reference to the symposion's songs of love occupy two separate areas, coordinating the aesthetic pleasure of sight with the musical expression of desire.

One last example will show how varied the graphic techniques could be for indicating speech and song. The tondo of a cup shows a youth walking forward holding a lyre and a drinking cup (fig. 104).[33] Behind him is a knobbed staff and the inscription that

[30] Red-figure amphora: Paris, Louvre G30; Beazley, ARV 15/9.
[31] Sappho, *ap. Etym. Mag.*, 485.43 (= fr. 6 App./36 Lobel-Page).
[32] Beazley, ARV 1591–1594.
[33] Red-figure cup: Erlangen, 454; Beazley, ARV 339/49. Join with Göttingen, H566i; Beazley, ARV 343/141 (D.J.R. Williams).

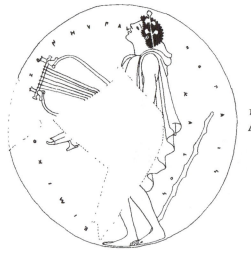

104. Red-figure cup,
Antiphon painter, ca. 480.

is so common, *ho pais kalos*, "the youth is beautiful," which could apply as easily to the figure in the painting as to another young man. The boy is singing, with his mouth open, but the inscription does not begin at his face as it did in our other examples; instead, it starts at his feet and rises toward his head, reading *eimi ko⟨ma⟩zon hupau . . .* , "I go forward, reveling, to the music of the flu[. . .]." The last word is cut off after the first syllable, as if it had not been completed by the singer. It can be restored either as *aulou*, "flute," or as *auleteros*, "flute player." The song envelops the young man, describes his activity, and embodies the meaning of the word *komos*, "festive procession," for *komazein* means to walk while singing and dancing, just as the youth in the tondo is doing. Poetry, like imagery, portrays the activity of the guests; this is a doubled self-portrait in both song and drawing. Once again this painting has an echo in Theognis—"When we have our feast, we may sing to the sound of a flute"—and in Hesiod—"The young men [. . .] proceed, in a happy company, to the rhythm of the flute."[34]

In all these images, the brief excerpt of poetry is either in the first person—"I am reveling; I desire; I can't"—or begins with a direct address—"O Apollo; o most beautiful; love, and . . ."—which implies a recipient, summoned by the vocative or the imper-

[34] Theognis, 825, 1065; Hesiod, *Aspis*, 281.

ative. In fact, the presence of a first or second person creates a situation that is typical of the symposion's lyric poetry,[35] which is primarily an act of communication among the guests. The exchange of poetic speech includes the whole group of drinkers, and, through the song, momentarily brings them together as an "I."

The poetry set into images in this way proclaims the pleasure of the symposion. Just as many images show a guest to the guests, an important part of archaic lyric is devoted to the symposion and to the very moment of its own recitation. The time for poetic performance and the place for the privileged reception of images coincide, putting into symmetry the reflective properties of song and imagery, both of which take their audience as their subject. In the several unusual examples we have analyzed, the inscription scarcely adds to our understanding of the image, which stands on its own; a written text *is* unusual because it is wholly unnecessary. Nonetheless, by making the guests' song visible, the painters integrate the acoustic into the visual and celebrate the verbal and musical content of the symposion.

The poetic themes suggested by the inscriptions are very close to those developed by archaic lyric, especially in Theognis. These are well worn, oft-repeated motifs, which allow for a great deal of improvisation.[36] The poem circulates among the guests in a relay, as they pass the lyre from hand to hand. Each one has enough poetic expertise to take up a familiar theme, recite a classic passage, or improvise for the occasion. There is a proverbial expression—"Not to know three by Stesichorus"—to describe a boor who is unable to quote three strophes by the great lyric poet. Education in Athens aimed at grounding the youths in poetry and music by teaching them to learn classical texts, drawn from the epic or lyric repertoire.

The painters sometimes show scenes of pedagogues using texts written on scrolls to train their pupils.[37] A fragment of a paint-

[35] See E. Benveniste, "L'Appareil formel de l'énonciation," 79–88.

[36] On the lyric motifs at the symposion, see G. Giangrande, "Sympotic Literature."

[37] See F. Beck, *Album of Greek Education* (Sydney, 1975). See also the articles by H. Immerwahr: "Book Rolls on Attic Vases," *Storia e Letteratura*, Studies in honor of Ullman, 1964, vol. 1, 17–48; "More Book Rolls on Attic Vases," *AntK* 16 (1973): 143–147.

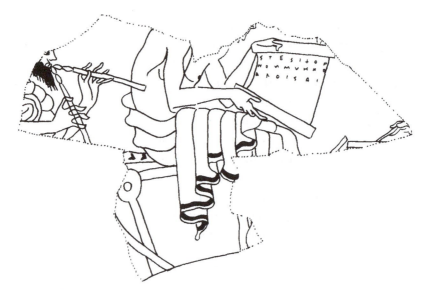

105. Red-figure cup, Onesimos, ca. 480.

ing shows a flute player to the left, a youth in the center holding a scroll, and a hand to the right holding a stylus and writing on a tablet (fig. 105).[38] In this case musical performance has a double relation to writing, which now (ca. 480) exists side by side with oral culture. The text on the scroll is completely legible, and the painter obviously wants to give the viewer of the vase a chance to read it. The writing does not run, as it should, from one cylinder to the other, for the youth holding it; instead it has been reoriented to the horizontal for the person looking at the painted scene. The text faces forward, so to speak, toward the outside of the image, while the youth is shown in profile, as is conventional at this time. The poem is written in the archaic style called *boustrophedon*, running first from left to right and then back across the page (see fig. 29). Moreover, the letters are also aligned in vertical columns, *stoichedon*, as in our crossword puzzles. Such a style of writing does not have readability as its chief goal—the words are not separated from one another—but strives for ornamental effect.[39] Once again the letter is a decoration. Still, it is quite easy to read the first line of a poem, *stesichoron*

[38] Red-figure cup: Oxford, G138.3, 5, 11; Beazley, ARV 326/93.
[39] On this style of writing, see R. P. Austin, *The Stoichedon Style in Greek Inscriptions* (Oxford, 1938).

106a. Red-figure cup, Douris, ca. 480.

106b. Red-figure cup (detail), Douris, ca. 480.

humnon agoisai: "[Muses?] guide the hymn that assembles the chorus."[40]

The same effect occurs on a cup by Douris that permits the viewer of the vase to read a written text held by a schoolmaster (figs. 106A,B).[41] Again, the figure is in profile while the scroll faces forward. It reads *moisa moi a{m}phi scamandron {eph}eur' on archomai aeide{i}n*: "Muse, find for me on the banks of the Scamander a place

[40] See J. D. Beazley, "Hymn to Hermes," AJA (1948): 337–338.
[41] Red-figure cup: Berlin, 2285; Beazley, ARV 431/48.

107. Red-figure cup, Brygos painter, ca. 480.

to start my song."[42] This is a line from epic, referring to the river
that ran through Troy, and the invocation to the Muse recalls those
we find in Homer or Hesiod. A boy stands in front of the teacher
and recites, and the written text serves to guide his performance. To
the left there is a music lesson, in which teacher and student practice
on the lyre. Musical accompaniment and recitation from memory
form a unit. In the field of the image there hang various accessories:
two lyres, a flute case, a basket, and also—surprisingly for a
school—two drinking cups. They are there as symbols of the symposion at which such musical apprenticeship is directed. This scene

[42] See F. Chamoux, "Un vers épique mal lu," *Rev. Philol.* (1970), 7–10, and a
forthcoming paper by C. Calame in *La part de l'oeil* 5 (1989).

is not a simple transcription of everyday life, such as it was; by including the two cups the painter clearly indicates the ultimate goal of the music and the song. The prominence of the poetic text foreshadows the delights of the symposia to come.

Image and song echo one another and come together in the symposion, where the senses combine, and "the sonorous flowing wine"[43] is heard. The conviviality of shared wine provides the locus for the development of musical and visual culture in archaic Athens. Many poets sang of Dionysus and extolled his gifts, sometimes drawing their inspiration from wine. Alcaeus, tradition says, wished to plant only a grapevine.[44] A fragment from Archilochus shows him in the grasp of Dionysus:

> I know how to sing the lovely hymn of lord Dionysus,
> the dithyramb, with my heart struck by wine.[45]

The god himself succumbs to musical ecstasy; the tondo of a cup (fig. 107) shows him holding a lyre, his head thrown back, flanked by two satyrs who dance while playing castanets and waving a vine branch that unfurls through the picture.[46] As Simonides proclaims, "Wine and music have the same source."[47]

[43] Philoxenus of Cythera *ap*. Athenaeus, 2.35d (= fr. 18/831 Page).
[44] Alcaeus *ap*. Athenaeus, 10.430c (= fr. Z18 Lobel-Page).
[45] Archilochus *ap*. Athenaeus, 14.628a (= fr. 120 West).
[46] Red-figure cup: Paris, Cabinet des médailles, 576; Beazley, ARV 371/14.
[47] Simonides *ap*. Athenaeus, 2.40a (= fr. 142/647 Page).

Epilogue

Drink to Me with Thine Eyes

In an elegy Critias gives a list of inventions that various nations have contributed to mankind: the Etruscans, gold and bronze vases; the Phoenicians, writing; and the Athenians, pottery:

> The city that raised the beautiful trophy at Marathon
> invented the potter's wheel and the oven and the child of clay,
> most renowned pottery, useful servant of the household.[1]

Athens' vases (*keramon*) are as much a part of her glory as is the victory at Marathon. This pottery, however, is not just the "useful servant of the household." Keramos is the son of Dionysus, and the painted vases are companions to the guests. They participate in the festivities of the symposion by embodying in their shape the ideal of circularity that controls relations among the guests. At times the potter's wheel stops being an artisan's tool and becomes a spectacular accessory to an acrobatic dance, as in Xenophon's *Symposium*.[2] It can also be a plaything for two satyrs (fig. 108), who hold onto each other's arms in centrifugal balance, as on a merry-go-round, which will make them as dizzy as does the god's wine.[3]

The vertigo produced by the dance is linked both to the

[1] Critias *ap.* Athenaeus, 1.28b (= 88 fr. B2 DK).
[2] Xenophon, *Symposium*, 7.2.
[3] Red-figure pelike: London, E387; Beazley, ARV 1134/10.

108. Red-figure pelike, manner of the Washing painter, ca. 450.

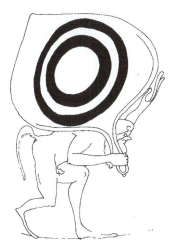

109. Black-figure olpe (detail), ca. 510.

110. Black-figure hydria, Eye-Siren group, ca. 530.

drunkenness caused by wine and to the fascination of the image, which plays off a wide range of effects: reflection, either mirrored or *en abyme*, an image that moves in the hands of the drinkers in the rich, distinctive setting of the symposion.

This extraordinary flexibility of the image should be emphasized again as we conclude; for our last example we may consider the metamorphoses of the eye under the painter's brush. The exterior of a cup may be decorated with large, staring eyes that make the vase into a kind of face (see fig. 37).[4]

---

[4] See G. Ferrari, "Eye Cups," *RA* (1986): 5–20.

111. Black-figure cup, painter of Cambridge 61, ca. 530.

Some vases go even farther and use the eye as a focus around which the other graphic elements are organized. Placing the eye over a simple curved line, like the deck of a ship, turns it into a sail for a voyage over the wine-dark sea.[5] A satyr can carry the eye on his back (fig. 109), like a wineskin full to bursting, the precious cargo of Dionysus.[6] The eye may be given a head, legs and tail to become a siren[7]—and at the same time, in magic doubling, it is a bird, a visual equivalent to the portmanteau words dear to Lewis Carroll (fig. 110). Even better, the pupil of the eye, which the Greeks call *kore* ("maiden"), may be replaced by the grimacing mask of the gor-

[5] Chalcidian black-figure cup: University of Zurich; *AntK* 26 (1983): 21, pl. 7.
[6] Black-figure olpe: Berkeley, *Lowie Museum of Anthropology*, 8.2163; Beazley, ABV 382/1.
[7] Black-figure hydria: London, B215; Beazley, ABV 286/1. See the black-figure cup: Boston, 10.651; Beazley, ABV 157/86.

goneion, to convey the fascinating power of the gaze that transfixes the drinker (fig. 111).[8]

That the eye is put through such a play of metamorphoses will come as no surprise. The vase painters are working in a setting in which wine, music, and image are complementary and, in their ties to one another, form a whole web of interrelations; at every level, metaphors and metamorphoses grow under the spell of Dionysus, master of illusion.

The artisans of the Kerameikos more than held their own in this culture, where vases are not mere trinkets tidily arranged on shelves, but objects that are almost alive, rich in meaning and poetry.

[8] Black-figure cup: Cambridge, Fitzwilliam Museum, 61 (GR39.1864); Beazley, ABV 202.2. See W. Deonna, "L'âme pupilline et quelques monuments figurés," *AC* 26 (1957): 59–90, and F. Frontisi-Ducroux, "In the Mirror of the Mask," 153–154, and figs. 212–214.

Sources of Illustrations

All the drawings in this volume are by the author. They are sketches based on the published documents, the references to which are to be found below and follow Beazley's system of abbreviations. These drawings do not pretend to replicate the stylistic quality of the originals: they are intended to facilitate the iconographic reading of the documents described, *procul ab urbe studentibus*. It seems unnecessary to repeat the notation "B.C." after all the dates—it is a given throughout.

1. New York 16.174.41; based on Richter-Hall pl. 35.
2. Cleveland 26.549; based on museum photograph.
3. Baltimore; based on CVA Robinson 2, pl. 2.
4. London 1910.2-12.1; based on JHS 1911.
5. Göttingen Univ. ZV 1964/ 139; photograph by D. Widmer.
6. Paris, Cabinet des médailles 320; B.N. photograph.
7. Würzburg 208; museum photograph.
8. Based on C. Börker; Festbankett und griechische Architektur, fig. 19.
9. New York 20.246; based on Richter-Hall pls. 53–54.
10. Brussels A 717; based on museum photograph.
11. Oxford 1965.127; museum photograph.
12. Paris, Louvre G459; based on Chuzeville photograph.
13. Karlsruhe 70/395; based on Thimme GV, fig. 39.
14. New York 07.286.84; based on FR, pl. 116.
15. London E351; based on museum photograph.
16. Paris, Louvre G71; based on Chuzeville photograph.
17. Berlin 2658; based on D.S. fig. 1429.

18. Berlin 2265; based on museum photograph.
19. Munich 2619A; based on FR, pl. 155.
20. Paris, Louvre G133; based on Chuzeville photograph.
21. Paris, Louvre G127; based on Hartwig, pl. 20.
22. Paris, Louvre G245; based on Chuzeville photograph.
23. Würzburg HA 166a; based on CVA 1, pl. 44.
24. Paris, Louvre G201; based on Chuzeville photograph.
25. Munich 2619A; based on FR, pl. 155.
26. Brussels A723; museum photograph.
27. New York 08.258.22; based on Richter-Hall, pl. 142.
28. Harvard 1960.236; A, based on AJA 1936; B, based on museum photograph.
29. London, British Museum; based on Boeckh, CIG, p. 8.
30. Paris, Louvre CA454; Chuzeville photograph.
31. Paris, Louvre CA454; based on *Recueil Pottier*, p. 227.
32. Baltimore, coll. Robinson; based on CVA 3, pl. 3.
33. Boston 95.16: A, author's photograph; B, based on CB 1, p. 34.
34. Boston 00.331; based on CVA 1, fig. 28.
35. Sarajevo 654; based on CVA 1, pl. 27.
36. Agrigento S65; based on museum photograph.
37. Oxford 1974.344; based on museum photograph.

38. New York 56.171.61; based on AA 1976, p. 288, fig. 9.
39. Naples H2948; author's photograph.
40. Boston 98.926; based on museum photograph.
41. Madrid II 267; based on Pfuhl, fig. 319.
42. Berlin 31 131; based on Hoppin 343.
43. Rome, Vatican 456; based on Albizzati, p. 208.
44. Limassol, Kakoyannis; based on BCH 1961.
45. Brussels R386; museum photograph.
46. Basel, market; photograph by D. Widmer.
47. See chapter 3, notes 36, 38–40.
48. Oxford 1965, 120; museum photograph.
49. Copenhagen 13 365; based on museum photograph.
50. Tübingen E41; based on Watinger, pl. 21.
51. Paris, Louvre G70; based on Chuzeville photograph.
52. Basel, BS463; photograph by D. Widmer.
53. New York 12.234.5; based on Richter-Hall, pl. 43.
54. Würzburg 471; based on Langlotz, pl. 140.
55. Paris, Louvre G92; based on Chuzeville photograph.
56. Brussels A723; based on museum photograph.
57. Cambridge 37.17; A, museum photograph; B, based on Pfuhl, fig. 343.
58. Providence 25.073; based on CVA, pl. 17.

59. Oberlin 67.61; photograph by D. Widmer.
60. Paris, Louvre F129; based on Chuzeville photograph.
61. Adria B471; based on CVA, pl. 7.
62. Paris, Louvre G73; based on Chuzeville photograph.
63. Tübingen S/10 1345 (E 54); based on Watzinger, pl. 25.
64. Berlin 2267; based on Hoppin 1, 149.
65. Boston 01.8024; based on Hartwig, pl. 5.
66. Paris, Louvre Cp 11072; based on Chuzeville photograph.
67. Berlin 2416; based on Annali 1876, pl. M.
68. Private collection; based on Vickers, fig. 17.
69. Leningrad 644; based on Klein, p. 105.
70. Munich 2421; based on FR, p. 71.
71. Paris, Louvre G114; based on Chuzeville photograph.
72. Florence, PD248; based on CVA, pl. 86.
73. Rome, Vatican; photograph by A. Held.
74. Rhodes 13 386; based on Clara Rhodos 4, 202.
75. Geneva 16 908; based on CVA 1, pl. 9.
76. Compiègne 1068; photograph by S. Hutin.
77. Athens 1045; based on AM 14, pls. 13–14.
78. Kassel, Dierichs collection; based on Gercke.
79. New York, market; photograph by D. Widmer.
80. New York 75.2.27 (GR593); based on Richter-Hall, pl. 152.
81. Berlin 2290; museum photograph.
82. Lucerne, market; based on Boardman ARFV, fig. 127.
83. Frankfurt; based on Bol, fig. 64.
84. Boston 99.515; based on author's photograph.
85. Rome, Vatican; based on Gerhard, pl. 109.
86. Boston 90.154; based on CVA 2, pl. 66.
87. London E22; museum photograph.
88. New York, Schimmel collection; based on Pantheon 23, 1965.
89. Palermo, Banco di Sicilia; based on Odeon, pl. 51.
90. Baltimore, Robinson collection; based on CVA 1, pl. 37.
91. Palermo 1518; based on Greifenhagen, Eroten, fig. 26.
92. Switzerland, private collection; based on Schefold, Meisterwerke no. 222.
93. Rome, Villa Giulia 64 608; based on E. Simon GV, pl. 61.
94. Munich 2044; museum photograph.
95. Munich 2416; based on FR, pl. 64.
96. Berlin inv. 1966.19; based on WZRostock 16, 1967, pl. 28.
97. Eleusis 907; based on BCH 108, 1984, p. 101, fig. 2a.
98. Elvejehm Museum of Art,

Madison 1979.122; based on
Moon-Berge no. 70.

99. Florence 3949; based on CVA
3, pl. 91.

100. Paris, Cabinet des médailles
546; based on Studies in
Honor of Robinson, pl. 25b.

101. Munich 2646; based on EAA
II, fig. 1128.

102. Athens, MN1357; based on
AM 9, 1884, pl. 1.

103. Paris, Louvre G30; based on
Chuzeville photograph.

104. Erlangen 454; based on
Hartwig, p. 256.

105. Oxford G138.3, 5, 11; based
on Immerwahr, Studies in
Honor of Ullman, fig. 1.

106. Berlin 2285, detail; based on
Rev. Philol. 1970; museum
photograph.

107. Paris, Cabinet des médailles
576; B.N. photograph.

108. London E387; based on Cecil
Smith, pl. 19.1.

109. Berkeley 8.2163; based on
museum photograph.

110. London B215; based on Elite
2, pl. 25.

111. Cambridge 61; museum
photograph.

Index

Lightning Source UK Ltd.
Milton Keynes UK
UKOW06f2210041214

242646UK00001B/12/P